LIVING IN TUSCANY

LIVING IN TUSCANY

Text by Leonardo Castellucci

Photographs by Gian Luigi Scarfiotti

Introduction by Lorenza de' Medici Stucchi

ABBEVILLE PRESS ◆ PUBLISHERS

New York ◆ London ◆ Paris

Text by Leonardo Castellucci
Photographs by Gian Luigi Scarfiotti
Introduction by Lorenza de' Medici Stucchi
Editor: Maria Luisa Viviani
Art Director: Giorgio Seppi

Copyright © 1991 Arnoldo Mondadori Editore S.p.A.,
Milan
English translation copyright © 1992 Arnoldo
Mondadori Editore S.p.A., Milan

Translated by Geoffrey Culverwell

Library of Congress Cataloguing-in-Publication Data

Castellucci, Leonardo.
    [Abitare in Toscana. English]
    Living in Tuscany / text by Leonardo
Castellucci; photography by Gian Luigi Scarfiotti.
        p. cm.
    Translation of: Abitare in Toscana.
    Includes index.
    ISBN 1-55859-320-9
    1. Architecture, Domestic--Italy--Tuscany--
Guide-books.   2. Interior decoration--Italy--
Tuscany--Themes, motives.
    I. Scarfiotti, Gian Luigi. II. Title.
    NA7356.T87C313 1992
    728'.0945'5--dc20   91-38153
                        CIP

First American Edition second printing

ISBN 1-55859-320-9
Printed and bound in Spain by Artes Gráficas Toledo, S.A.
D.L. TO: 598-1994

CONTENTS

INTRODUCTION

Those who choose to live in Tuscany today rarely do so just to contemplate its beauty; its culture has a richness and variety that call for understanding, love and respect. Whether a person has been born and bred in Tuscany or has recently arrived, whether they live in an abbey in Chianti, a castle in the Casentino, a rambling house in the Maremma, an old seigneurial villa in the Lucchesia, or an idyllic farmhouse in Siena, they are all participating in an exciting moment in the history of the Tuscan countryside. Even the newest arrivals gradually find themselves being turned into natives. Maybe they are searching for pleasure in its most complete form or just desire a quality of life not found elsewhere, a joie de vivre that keeps those who have always lived there and attracts those who have decided to start a new life.

What is certain is that these new settlers represent a revolutionary development for an area whose

inhabitants lived such harsh lives in the not too distant past. A strong concept of tradition produced the deep-rooted culture of Tuscany where beauty is not simply the expression of a contrived aesthetic, but the outcome of a harsh struggle to bring every possible piece of land into cultivation. The harmonious balance between the natural beauty of the land and the skilful handiwork of man has been achieved by the slow and patient work of a people who, generation after generation, have tended the

fields and transformed the face of the land into a perfect pathway of cypresses, fields, vineyards, woods and gardens that lead one into another with no precise boundaries.

Over the years, however, the peasants' life became too hard, the gap between the yield of the soil and the number of hungry mouths to feed too great, so that for many the lure of the city proved irresistible. The land was abandoned as people fled, and the entire region fell into a deep crisis. Those who remained and continued to believe in the land with a stubborn pride have been rewarded with a leading role in the birth and rebirth of many flourishing enterprises. Their success has attracted the attention of people all over the world who understand the region's potential. Businessmen and owners of large companies have in particular spent considerable sums of money on restoring villas and country houses of every shape and size. Many of them have also invested in land, in vineyards and olive groves, fuelling the phenomenon of new farmers, who now exist side by side with the noble families that traditionally owned the land. The newcomers are devoting their efforts to the region's most famous products, such as oil and wine, finding ingenious ways of improving production. As a result, some of the more astute and far-seeing producers have made changes in the wine-making sector, re-examining and abandoning some traditional practises in their search for new methods. Their experiments have yielded wines able to compete successfully with the products of France and California.

A similar growth in the arts and entertainment has brought fame to the places where festivals, shows, concerts and exhibitions are held. This is especially evident during the warmer months as an

international summer population drifts through villages, piazzas, villas, abbeys and private or public gardens, perhaps to watch an English troupe perform an eccentric opera in a restored convent; or to dance to the gentle sound of an accordion celebrating the patron saint of a tiny hamlet lost amongst the hills of Chianti; or to laugh at a donkey race while feasting on the small, anise-flavoured wafers known as brigidini; or to enjoy an elegant concert in one of the small towns around Arrezzo; or to swim in the Parco dell'Uccellina; or to attend one of the elegant dinners of Siena's Accademici della Cucina Italiana; or to take a night-time visit to a natural spring; or to imbibe at a wine tasting at a friend's cellar; or to celebrate a new neighbourhood restaurant that has just opened up.

The happy throng moves through the sultry summer heat eager to live life to its fullest.

Life today in the Tuscan countryside is a wonderful feast, with everything conspiring to please the senses: the people, the works of art, the seasons, the landscape, the festivals, the tastes, the smells. Autumn and winter are the seasons when life slows down its pace and becomes a little solitary, affording a moment for reflection and rest after the hectic activity of the summer. But no matter what time of year it happens to be, Tuscany offers the chance to enjoy beauty in its fullest sense, to understand how a love of life and a thirst for knowledge ensured the survival of this beautiful land with its gentle civilization and its great traditions.

Lorenza de' Medici Stucchi

VILLAS

The villas of Tuscany, whether of great architectural beauty, or of more modest pretensions, have always been symbols of wealth and opulence. They are scattered throughout the region: the Medici villas in the province of Florence, the Sienese ones made of brick, the characteristic building material of Siena, and, above all, the ones around Lucca – true masterpieces of the builder's art.

VILLA DI CAPEZZANA

The most striking feature of the splendid Villa di Capezzana is the perfect placement of decor throughout the house. Here we see an abstract, aesthetically composed corner of the *sala grande*, (main reception room) an arrangement based on perfect symmetry, an exercise in purity. Beneath the painting stands a finely carved pedestal, and to each side identical chairs mark the borders of the picture. The image shows Bacchus, overcome by wine, eyes glazed and staring, body fleshy and legs unsteady. He is held up by an ass bearing bunches of grapes and by a young boy struggling to carry the weight. The painting comes from the brush of Sebastiano Ricci, one of the greatest seventeenth–eighteenth-century Italian painters, whose inspired genius can be appreciated in famous galleries throughout the world.

Access to the villa is via a winding avenue flanked with slender cypresses. A stone's throw away is Poggio a Caiano, a town in the heart of "Medici villa" country. And the Villa di Capezzana is indeed a Medici villa, commissioned between the end of the fifteenth and the beginning of the sixteenth century by this powerful Florentine family, who presented it to one

Above: In the *sala grande* an eighteenth-century pedestal is flanked by two chairs in the Tuscan style. Above them hangs Sebastiano Ricci's *Bacchus*, impressive in its technique and its iconography.

Opposite: An overview of the *sala grande*, a typical example of an aristocratic Tuscan interior. The room contains a number of fine paintings; the one on the right is *Landscape with Ancient Monuments and Figures* by Alessandro Magnasco and Marco Ricci, two eighteenth-century Italian masters. A beautiful coffered wood ceiling covers this vast hall, off which other rooms form a concentric pattern. A nineteenth-century Persian carpet covers much of the paved floor.

of their daughters on the occasion of her marriage.

But for many centuries there must have been another, much older building on the site; a Latin document of A.D. 804 records that there were already extensive vineyards and olive groves. The Medici were the first owners, followed by the marchesi Bourbon del Monte, the conti Adimari Morelli, the baroni Franchetti, and finally the conti Contini Bonaccossi, the present owners.

The villa is broad and solid. Its clean lines reflect the stylistic preferences of contemporary Tuscan architecture and the design projects a feeling of deftness and certainty. The arrangement of rooms gives its internal layout a strong rational quality. The main facade at the end of the great entrance courtyard stands in a small world of its own, enclosed within a delicate wall. Beyond the facade stands a range of ancient granaries, one of which has been transformed into a garage, while another has assumed the role of a large recreation room. The lemon house, however, still awaits the many plants that it will shelter during the winter months.

As though to instill a feeling of respect, four marble statues of Atlas, with grim

Above: The outer and inner facades display a simple, symmetrical elegance. An old well stands at the center of the courtyard, while a small rose garden, carefully tended by the contessa Contini Bonaccossi, welcomes visitors with its feeling of space and light. The area serves as a terrace looking out over the surrounding countryside.

Right: One of the four eighteenth-century statues of Atlas, the mythological Titan and father of the Pleiades, condemned by Zeus to carry the world on his shoulders.

The Tuscan landscape is by no means uniform. Sometimes it gives an impression of gentle lushness, sometimes of harsh scrubbiness, while at other times it is a combination of the two. The countryside around the Villa di Capezzana is gentle, with swelling hills scored by tracks and dusty paths, while rows of cypresses and small patches of trees lap the edges of the road leading from Florence to Pistoia. It is a harmonious landscape, an example of how humans can make a mark on nature without changing it, but simply "training" it into a pleasing order.

faces and rippling muscles, mark the entrance to the *piano nobile* (the principal storey of the building). These statues, from the Villa Reale at Monza, were acquired by Alessandro Contini Bonaccossi during the early years of this century. Today, the villa's master is Alessandro's grandson, Count Ugo, who is every inch a gentleman, a gracious host and a producer of fine wines.

The first room to greet the visitor is the *sala grande*. It is here that Ricci's painting of Bacchus hangs, as well as a landscape attributed to the eighteenth-century artists Marco Ricci and Alessandro Magnasco.

A large rectangular rug covers almost the entire paved floor, while the walls are dotted with other paintings and prints. There is also a tiny yet charming *salotto* (drawing room), whose focal point is a French gilt mirror and table, a riot of carved wooden flowers. Other items of furniture include a small table, a very inviting sofa and two comfortable armchairs that are all in perfect keeping with the mood of the room. This leads into the restful *salottino Impero*, which is opened up only for guests. Its furniture – the envy of any antique dealer – includes a circular occasional table, small side tables, an impressive collection of other pieces made of precious woods and an enigmatic portrait of an eighteenth-century worthy. Everything possesses an elegant stylistic coherence, even the simple decorations that frame certain corners of the room.

The *stanza di Elena*, an eccentric bedroom with two solid brass beds, was decorated during the early twentieth century on the occasion of an illustrious marriage in the Bourbon del Monte family. Its walls are adorned with sprays of roses and flowered swags painted in a simple, spontaneous style. Swans and herons swooping in graceful flight garland the ceiling with flowered ribbons grasped in their beaks.

The severe, inner facade is lightened by a simple and unassuming garden: a massed bed of flowering roses and hydrangeas. A small area paved with terracotta tiles is flanked by a low wall leading into the terrace that acts as a balcony overlooking the typical Tuscan landscape, dotted with trees.

In the spacious courtyard two boister-

Above: The villa's old stables have been turned into a large room in which old furniture, famous paintings, and even ledgers recording daily family expenditures are kept in apparent "disorder."

Opposite: A highly original piece of early-nineteenth-century Luccan furniture, a perfect combination of practicality and ingenuity.

Below: The nineteenth-century mantelpiece is just one of the elements in the restrained and elegant setting of the *salottino*.

ous sheepdogs beg for attention, surrounded by a comforting silence broken only by the quiet sounds of everyday life. It is an idyllic scene that matches the gracious mood of the villa.

Beyond the door of what were once the villa's stables is a room that looks for all the world like a scene from a Visconti film. Very different from the rooms already described, it lacks their "museum-like" quality, their formal elegance and their decorative purity, but is nevertheless very welcoming; its "lived-in" appearance conveys an atmosphere both contrived and yet spontaneous. Everything conspires to make this room a veritable storehouse of memories: the family photographs, the piles of books and magazines on the table, the attractive piece of mirrored furniture in the Empire style, the original and highly ingenious early-nineteenth-century Luccan piece with its veritable maze of hidden drawers and small shelves that open in every direction, the display cabinet in the English style and two old ledgers that list with meticulous precision all the expenses incurred from the eighteenth century up to the present. The room seems almost like an antique shop, a place in which things appear to have been randomly arranged with a sense of impermanence and with no real attempt at conventional furnishing.

On one wall a young Japanese girl in a

multicoloured costume gazes down at us. This is the famous *Ritratto di Asiatica (Portrait of an Eastern girl)*, painted by Primo Conti in 1924; the companion piece hangs in the Museum of Modern Art in Florence's Palazzo Pitti. On another wall a second splendid canvas can be glimpsed, hanging casually above a Tuscan chest. This famous painting, Tintoretto's *Self-Portrait with Mother and Father* – which could well hang in the Uffizi Gallery – is immediately recognizable, but the use of both masterpieces as just another part of the room's decoration is in itself a very bold and successful treatment. The large room in which they hang is divided by a wall containing two arches and is filled with light streaming in from the small adjoining courtyard, creating a feeling of airiness as it floods across the paved floor and bounces off the furniture in thin shafts.

Every evening, throughout the changing seasons of the year, the villa is the scene of an age-old domestic ritual, a custom hallowed by time, as Count Ugo closes the gates and inspects the house, always accompanied by the melancholy sheepdogs. These powerful animals are the faithful guardians of the villa, which acts as a link with the memory of the old lords of Tuscany.

The estate's vineyards are equally ancient and equally venerable. The Capezzana red wines, for which the estate

Above: This room has a "classic" mood, with a divan more than two centuries old and a large mirror above the fireplace.

Opposite: Glowing fields of sunflowers dot the Tuscan landscape.

Below: The *salottino*, which leads off the entrance hall, features a spectacular hand-carved and gilt French mirror whose exuberance contrasts strongly with the general mood of linearity.

is renowned, are famous throughout the world. They are produced with every attention to detail (within the courtyard is an apartment reserved for the resident oenologist), the product of constant research, of a continuous process of refinement. One of the many wines produced by these vineyards recently won a major international prize. The reds include Villa di Capezzana, Villa di Capezzana Riserva and Villa di Trefano, made with a generous proportion of the Sangiovese grape, with a ruby-red colour verging on garnet, an intense bouquet and a mellow, velvety taste. Another, more recent introduction is Vin Ruspo, a self-confident rosé with a fresh, fruity dryness. The estate's pride and joy, however, are its Capezzana and Capezzana Chianti Montalbano, two aristocrats of the wine world, both of which have been granted the D.O.C.G. appellation.

The white wines, whose quality is in no way inferior to the reds, include Capezzana Bianco and Capezzana Chardonnay, which are both in great demand by the most discerning palates. The sparkling Tenuta di Capezzana Brut, very few bottles of which are produced each year, is another great source of pride for the conti Contini Bonaccossi, as is their Vin Santo, Tuscany's best-known dessert wine. And the estate is not known just for its wines: Capezzana's extra-virgin olive oil, produced with the proper, time-

Left: In the spacious environment that once housed the stables, a large table is piled high with books, magazines and other clutter. In accordance with the philosophy of its owners, the sixteenth-century masterpiece *Self-Portrait with Mother and Father* by Tintoretto is treated like just another decorative element. The *cassettone* is a particularly fine example of nineteenth-century Tuscan furniture.

Opposite: The unique decoration of the *stanza di Elena* was created on the occasion of a wedding. The painted ceiling is particularly fine.

Overleaf: Tuscany is not always green; some areas have a dry, almost lunar landscape.

Below: This nineteenth-century English display cabinet houses a collection of porcelain.

honoured method of cold pressing, is equally famous.

These achievements are the result of a combination of many different factors: a land almost constantly exposed to the sun, experience born of both tradition and continuous experimentation, and, most important of all, a great love of the work. All his life Count Ugo has devoted himself to wine, which he believes has a soul and a spirit of its own. It therefore becomes the duty of those involved in its creation to find the elements needed to make it not merely a wine but a great wine. And so every year, after the grape harvest, great efforts are made at the villa to bring out the best characteristics of the grape and thus of the wine that is to come. It is a challenge taken up every year, a wager constantly made with nature.

VILLA ROSPIGLIOSI

This is the story of a villa, a pope and a great architect that unfolds between 1667 and 1669, the years during which the papacy rested in the hands of Giulio Rospigliosi, a member of a family of ancient lineage that boasted vast estates in the Lamporecchio area near Pistoia.

Giulio had been singled out for an ecclesiastical career from an early age. Being an ambitious but also genuinely devout man, he readily accepted this decision and in 1667 he ascended the papal throne, adopting the name of Clement IX. The vast estate he already owned at Spicchio did not seem impressive enough for a pope, so he asked the greatest Roman architect of the day, Gianlorenzo Bernini, to draw up plans for a new villa. Almost as if he had a premonition of his impending death, he stipulated that the villa was to be completed in the shortest time possible. The work was actually undertaken by Mattia de' Rossi, one of Bernini's greatest pupils. According to Pascoli, a noted historian of the day, it appears that de' Rossi "had likewise been commissioned to draw up designs for a palace, which His Holiness wanted built at a villa of his at Lamporecchio ... and after Bernini had com-

Above: Pope Clement IX Rospigliosi's ornate coat of arms hangs above the entrance on the villa's main facade. It symbolizes the nobility and power of a family that owned vast estates in the surrounding countryside.

Opposite: Today, the magical *salone delle feste* is used by the villa's owner, Renzo Taddei, for receptions and cocktail parties. Its pale, glowing colours give the room a feeling of great light. The female figures around the base of the vault represent the signs of the zodiac, while above them soars the chariot of the sun, an allegory found in many other wealthy houses as a symbol of the power of the family who had commissioned it.

pleted them, Mattia was sent there to build it.'' It may thus have been Bernini himself who planned the building, which would be highly significant, given the fact that there are so few testaments to his genius in Tuscany.

But Clement IX passed away in 1669, so he never saw the finished building, which was finally completed around 1678. It is an impressive complex of very elegant lines, consisting of a central block enclosed by two projecting wings. The original facade, however, was much lighter and less bulky in appearance; instead of the modern roof, a broad balustrade – removed during the eighteenth century – crowned the top floor. The original drawings have survived, however, and they provide a much more pleasing and certainly less forbidding image than the one that confronts us today. The villa is now owned by Renzo Taddei, the famous restaurateur of the nearby spa town of Montecatini.

At the center of the broad expanse of lawn lies an ornamental pond containing a statue of a satyr, or perhaps the lascivious woodland deity Pan, holding pipes and resting on a raft of pebbles.

The large windows, outlined by

Left: This delicately intimate picture, depicting the Madonna and Child with the young Saint John, is borne aloft by two cherubs. It hangs in a small frescoed chapel next to the great reception hall.

Below: This elegant fresco shows four horses drawing Apollo's chariot through the heavens, while around the edges a number of putti disport themselves. The fresco, which dates from the early nineteenth century, is framed by fine plasterwork.

strongly shaped stone, impart a feeling of severity to the facade. Inside, the dramatic oval of the great hall is entirely covered in light-hearted frescoes. One cycle of frescoes, completed at the end of the seventeenth century on the occasion of a marriage between one of the Rospigliosi sons and a girl from the Pallavacini family, is a graceful representation of the signs of the zodiac, portrayed as female figures wearing crowns of laurel and garlands. All around, delicate winged putti soar playfully into the air, suspended amid swags of multicoloured flowers and sharing, with their joyful innocence, in the marriage celebrations. The ceiling fresco, which dates from almost a hundred years later, depicts the chariot of the sun, a recurring image in the frescoes of eighteenth-century villas and one that was intended to underline the magnificence of the buildings' noble owners.

Right: The main facade of the Villa Rospigliosi, designed by Gianlorenzo Bernini, is remarkable for the way in which the central section is set back between two wings. In the foreground is an ornamental pond, the centerpiece of a large lawn that was once an Italian garden. Bernini's career as an architect reached its peak with his design for Saint Peter's Square in Rome (1656–67), a trapezoidal space in front of the basilica with two colonnades enclosing the oval square. It is a brilliant solution that perfectly counterbalances the breadth of the facade.

The labyrinth of rooms, both large and small, carries on at the mezzanine level, where there is another vast space, this time undecorated, which repeats the shape of the entrance hall. From the air the villa's groundplan appears as a large H, and it is interesting to compare this shape with that of the famous Palazzo Barberini in Rome, another of Bernini's masterpieces. The same H-shaped layout is repeated in the dignified family chapel facing the villa on the other side of the garden, which suggests that this building too was designed by the same architect. Its structural elements are enlivened by the use of dark stonework juxtaposed with areas of pale plaster. Dedicated to Saints Simon and Jude, it contains frescoes that were probably created by artists of the Roman school during the second half of the eighteenth century. The rear facade of the villa, identical to the main

Left: A perspective view of the villa's entrance, with its broad, low flight of steps leading to a balustrade and a terrace overlooking the lawns. The doorway, dominated by the coat of arms of Pope Clement IX Rospigliosi, opens into the great reception hall, while the glazed door opposite leads into the park, which is fringed by olive groves.

Opposite: From the windows of the upper floor visitors can look over the lawn and admire the view of the family chapel, also the work of the great Roman architect. This little building, which contains a small cycle of frescoes that is probably the work of the mid-eighteenth-century Roman School, is perfectly in keeping with the splendours of the villa.

Below: One of the two statues from the balustrade: a guard dog, possibly a mastiff, protecting the entrance to the villa.

one, overlooks a park crossed by a long, tree-lined avenue that cuts through the green of the surrounding landscape, composed mainly of rustic olive groves.

The villa, rechristened ''la Rospigliosa'' or ''la villa del Papa'' by the locals, is a pontiff's dream come true, an architectural masterpiece by a great artist combined with the work of the area's inhabitants, who have always regarded it with awe and affection. For them ''la Rospigliosa'' is not just a beautiful seventeenth-century villa, but a source of prestige, of satisfaction, and of pride, a monument that makes them feel as though they are the children of an illustrious and living past.

VILLA MARIA TERESA

Just a few miles from the ancient Tuscan city of Lucca is a lush landscape with rolling hills and gentle streams that water the surrounding land. The countryside here abounds in architecturally breathtaking villas built during the centuries of Lucca's greatest prosperity.

The Villa di Borbone, better known by the name of its first owner, Maria Teresa of Savoy, is one such villa, with an elegant yet solid design and an admirable austerity. It is one of the many buildings created by Lorenzo Nottolini, one of the most famous Italian architects of the early nineteenth century. Maria Teresa, the wife of Carlo Ludovico di Borbone, who was son of Maria Luisa, Duchess of Lucca, was a quiet and pious woman whose memory still lives on in the villa's lack of ostentation.

Today the villa belongs to the Rossi di Montelera family, with the contessa Immacolata Rossi di Montelera, daughter of the artist Gregorio Calvi di Bergolo, as the careful custodian and chatelaine. Although she herself is not a painter, she has inherited her father's artistic gifts. A patron of the arts, she is an astute and sensitive promoter both of established artists and of those whose work is still not

Above: Sited on a small hill, the Villa Maria Teresa dominates the fertile Luccan landscape of olive groves and flourishing vineyards. At a distance it appears to be enclosed by a stone balcony, which on closer inspection proves to be a walled terrace containing a highly unusual garden.

Opposite: The rear facade of the nineteenth-century villa is fringed by an elegant garden containing rectangular beds edged with box and filled with flowers. The decorative marble urns are the only non-naturalistic elements in the garden.

widely known. The artists live and work at the villa, keeping alive the link between the mistress of the house and the world of painting, marble, sculpture, ideas, feelings and traditions.

A solid, expansive structure, the villa is arranged on three floors. The entrance is surrounded by four Ionic columns, like a temple gateway; a band of decoration running along the top of the wall is composed of crosses, symbols of the House of Savoy and the legend "Fert."

Two identical buildings stand at the entrance to the property, their architectural elements echoing those of the villa. One of them used to house the stables, while the other acted as a guard house. The villa is a few steps away, set in a garden filled with a variety of contrasting delights: large pots of gardenias, azaleas and geraniums, geometric beds ranged around a fountain in the Empire style, a clump of tall bay trees, a compact Italianate garden with a strong geometrical quality, a few long green lines of box bushes facing the countryside, tall trees, a spreading cedar of Lebanon, an old palm (reminder of a past taste for the exotic) and a statue of Venus, copied by the great Canova from the classical

original. Despite its varied inspiration, the garden conveys a sense of tranquil harmony.

Once through the main door, the motif of Ionic columns is repeated, this time with a more theatrical note, creating the feeling of a stage awaiting its actors. The elegant staircase is embellished with two small Empire-style tables and, on the walls, two large seventeenth-century canvases of battle scenes that capture the

Opposite above: The villa's monumental entrance features a doorway flanked by four Ionic columns in marble. The effect is one of restraint and elegance.

Opposite below: In one corner of the grounds stands a small drinking fountain, long since dried up.

Left: On clear days it is possible to catch a distant glimpse of the sea beyond the rolling hills.

Below: The entrance leads into this majestic neoclassical hallway where the column motif is repeated, echoing the monumental style of the facade. The most widely used decorative material is marble, which recurs in the columns, a number of tables and also certain internal and external details. The large canvas, which possesses an ''unfinished'' quality, provides a clever yet harmonious contrast between the old and the new.

most dramatic moment of the struggle, with the field a tangle of men and horses.

The ballroom is shrouded in shadow; an eighteenth-century table and a lively seventeenth-century Italian painting are visible through the gloom. In one corner is a softly lit piano, while an eighteenth-century still life provides a detailed portrayal of carnations, lilies, chrysanthemums and roses. The focal point of the *salotto* is provided by two small sofas that catch the light streaming through the window. Three canvases by Savinio, almost a homage to Seurat, are displayed casually on the wall, as is a fine Renaissance-revival-style painting by Vito Tongiani, with its background of a real yet timeless landscape and foreground depicting two large human figures with an almost symmetrical quality.

Beyond lie a number of other rooms, the most memorable of which include a bedroom decorated in the Empire style and another with two beds of highly imaginative design accompanied by elegant early-nineteenth-century velvet and gilt armchairs and an attractive contemporary screen. Looking out from the villa we can take a lingering look over the magical Luccan countryside bathed in sunlight.

The Villa Maria Teresa is universally regarded as a pioneer in the production of wine because the Rossi di Montelera family have adopted quality as their watchword. The olive oil from the estate

Above: Other rooms lead off the *salotto*, among them this bedroom with its decorated ceiling, bed, small dresser and cheval glass in an Empire style.

Opposite: The first room we encounter on the upper floor is this welcoming *salotto* that leads on to the balcony in the rear facade, from which it is possible to admire the gardens and enjoy a panoramic view over the surrounding countryside. The contessa Immacolata Rossi di Montelera's interest in painting and art in general is clearly evidenced by the numerous paintings on the walls, the most striking of which are three works by Savinio, all revealing the influence of Seurat. The unostentatiously elegant *salotto* is further enhanced by the decorations that run around the edges of the ceiling and frame the doorways. With its modern sofas upholstered in fabrics woven by Luccan craftsmen, the *salotto* is the contessa's favourite room, and it is here that she often entertains her literary friends and artists.

is also produced using traditional techniques. The conti Rossi di Montelera personally supervise the running of the wine business, which is one of the best in the Lucchesia. The villa's beautiful brick-vaulted wine cellars are run along the most modern lines yet with a concern for traditional values. They produce two types of wine: a white and a red typical of the Luccan hills. The oenologist in charge of the wine-making process lives a short distance from the property and constantly keeps an eye on the wines' development. The red is produced using a gentle pressing of the grapes and fermentation at a carefully controlled temperature, a long and laborious process, but one that provides a guarantee of quality. Particular care is taken with the casks in which the wine is aged, which, as decreed by tradition, are only used at the peak of condition. The wine cellars also possess the old-fashioned wooden casks, which, although making the process more expensive, always ensure excellent results.

VILLA MANSI

The grounds of the Villa Mansi are classically beautiful. There is a large, open lawn and a small shrubbery sheltering beneath a broad canopy of trees. A few steps away we encounter a hidden grotto, in whose pool stands the perfectly formed figure of the goddess Diana, modestly covering her breast with one hand as she invites her reluctant companion to join her in the water. It is a graceful sculptural composition, made even more striking by its rustic setting.

A little further on, the pond of elegantly irregular shape surrounded by a balcony of small columns is the work of the great architect Filippo Juvarra, who was also responsible for the grotto of Diana.

In the background, the fairy-tale facade of the villa emerges from behind the trees, finally revealing itself in all its glory. One of the most important villas in the Lucca region, the Villa Mansi displays a strong sense of movement in its fine portico composed of columns linked alternately by arches and architraves, with a symmetrical staircase leading to the entrance and to the statues adorning the central section of the facade.

Already in existence during the sixteenth century, the villa was extensively

Above: During the eighteenth century the architect and designer Filippo Juvarra planned this garden on formal Italian lines, but his original design was lost during the nineteenth century. This romantic pond surrounded by a low balustrade is a survival of Juvarra's original layout, as is the evocative grotto of Diana found nearby.

Opposite: The sumptuous ballroom has a dramatic, fairy-tale quality. Gilded decoration frames paintings and frescoes from the neoclassical era, while large eighteenth-century chandeliers flood the floor with light. The room is an allegorical display of wealth and power.

altered by the Urbino architect Muzio Oddi, who between 1634 and 1635 supervised a project involving the complete renovation of the facade and part of the main fabric of the building. At that time the villa belonged to the ancient Cenami family, who sold it to the Mansi family in 1675. Today it belongs to the contessa Laura Mansi, the last descendant of the branch of the family that owns the villa.

The Villa Mansi is famed for the elegance of its architecture, but it is equally famous for the stories of the ghostly figure of a woman which has apparently been sighted more than once around the edge of the pond. A benign presence who seems to favour clear, starry nights when the grounds of the villa are bathed in pale moonlight, she is the ghost of one of its most illustrious mistresses, Lucida Samminiati, the second wife of Gaspare Mansi. The present owners make light of the apparition and give little credence to this supposed spirit of one of their ancestors, but there are many locals who are more than prepared to swear to the contrary.

Lucida Mansi is the central figure of a fascinating tale, one reminiscent of old Doctor Faustus. The young Lucida was a lively, pretty girl who lived a life of

VILLA MANSI

Preceeding spread: Beyond a vast green expanse of lawn, against a backdrop of trees, the Villa Mansi appears in all its glory. A pillared portico and a symmetrical stairway enhance the sense of architectural unity, further embellished with many statues.

Left: Two glimpses of the monumental portico; between two Doric columns stands one of the many statues that adorn the facade.

Opposite: Another glimpse of the ballroom showing a fine eighteenth-century marble-topped table and a canvas by classicist painter Stefano Tofanelli, who was also responsible for the other paintings adorning the walls and ceiling of the room.

Below: The ceiling of the ballroom is decorated with frescoes depicting mythological and allegorical figures. These naked male statues, executed with a fine sense of perspective, seem to be supporting two pilasters.

luxury in a large palazzo in Lucca. Rather vain, she had a horror of growing old and of seeing her incomparable beauty wither. Obsessed by the need to keep a constant eye on every part of her body, she had the whole of her bedroom lined with mirrors. But time marched relentlessly on and so Lucida, like Faustus, called on the devil for his sinister help. He was happy to oblige, and granted her thirty years of unchanging beauty in

exchange for her soul. They were glorious years for the lady; as time passed she remained eternally youthful, even more beautiful than ever. But when her allotted time was over, she was carried away in a whirlwind from her country villa here at Segromigno. Since then her spirit has wandered abroad, unable to find repose.

The truth, however, is somewhat different: Lucida Mansi died of the plague in the mid seventeenth century and was buried in the now-vanished Capuchin church. But people still see her today.

The rooms on the *piano nobile* follow one after the other in pleasing symmetry, with a large ballroom at the center and a series of other rooms leading off either side. Following several thefts, furnishings have for some time been kept to a minimum, and the owners have been obliged to place all their remaining valuables in safekeeping. Even so, the ballroom has a magnificent fresco decoration, with a fine eighteenth-century gilded table and, most significantly, a number of large canvases crowding the walls and ceiling. These beautiful works by the classicist painter Stefano Tofanelli include, on the two walls, *The Judgement of Midas* and *The Death of Marsyas*, and, above each of the four doors, Apollo with Daphne, Hyacinthus, Coronis and Cyparissus. The ceiling depicts *The Triumph of Apollo*, who is shown driving a winged chariot drawn by slender, muscular horses

Opposite and above: On the *piano nobile* a large number of rooms lead off the central ballroom, among them this sumptuous bedroom with an eighteenth-century canopied bed. The series of fantastic decorations running around the walls culminate in the poetic fresco seen above, the work of an unknown hand, but which can be dated to the eighteenth century.

Below: The same room seen from a different angle. The raking light enters through a door which leads on to the portico overlooking the garden, visible from every part of the villa.

straining gracefully in the air as they carry the god towards the sun.

One room, which looks on to the portico, houses an elegant canopied bed of the eighteenth-century Italian school. The walls are adorned with fantastic decoration and the ceiling bears a charming fresco of an angel surrounded by winged putti in the midst of the vast blue heavens.

The villa blends perfectly into its parkland garden. The overall style is a mixture of the rococo and the baroque. Until the last century the lawns contained small Italianate beds laid out in an original geometric pattern designed by Juvarra, who was also responsible for certain elements of the villa. During the nineteenth century, however, these were replaced by a landscaped garden in the English style. As a result, the villa at Segromigno now stands in a vast park, although certain corners containing decorative statues and Italianate beds still survive today.

The park, the memories of Muzio Oddi and Filippo Juvarra, the haunting presence of Lucida Mansi, and the elegant statues scattered between the house and its grounds, all contribute to the magic of the Villa Mansi.

VILLA DI CAMUGLIANO

Pheasants stroll slowly about the grass, pecking at the greenery, then suddenly they stretch out their necks and scuttle off to safety as fast as their thin legs will carry them. The grass, which later gives on to a large, almost circular lawn, is empty once again. At its center stands a fine statue depicting the muscular figure of Hercules raising a club threateningly into the air, about to strike his victim.

In the background stands the solid and reassuring facade of the Villa di Camugliano, situated near Ponsacco, a short distance from Pisa. A sturdy building, with towers at each corner which look as if they are holding it up, it is a happy blend of a noble country house and a fortified stronghold.

The young marchese Lorenzo Niccolini, and his wife, Alessandra Marcello, have chosen to settle on this property, which has been in the Niccolini family since 1637, when one of the Lorenzo's illustrious ancestors, the senator Filippo Niccolini, acquired it from Cosimo II de' Medici.

In fact, the villa and its vast estate originally belonged to the grand dukes of Tuscany, who had it erected as a bastion against the separatist stirrings of the im-

Above: A glimpse of the large lawn that extends all the way to the surrounding woodland.

Opposite: The Medici Villa di Camugliano has been in the marchese Niccolini's family for several centuries. Although an elegant country home, the four corner towers proclaim its ancient role as a fortified stronghold. The villa, which dates from the sixteenth century, did not gain its residential appearance until 1637, when a number of elegant additions were made, both inside and out, such as the beautiful staircase leading up to the main door. The fine marble sculpture at the center of the lawn is the only decorative element on this large sweep of green, which is often visited by the splendid pheasants the Niccolinis enjoy breeding.

poverished but still bellicose Pisans. It was in 1533 that Alessandro de' Medici commissioned the building of a fortified villa at Camugliano, which was completed during the time of Cosimo I. This great complex, certainly a noble edifice, was the scene of frequent visits by the Medici, but, above all, it acted as a watchtower overlooking the winding valleys of the Era and the Casciana. It was an ideal vantage point, well equipped to cope with any military incursions, as is witnessed by the two large buildings standing at the end of the garden that were once used to house the grand duke's troops. Presented by Cosimo to his faithful friend Giuliano Gondi, the villa was subsequently acquired by the marchese Matteo Botti.

Shortly afterwards, in 1620, this family surrendered it to Grand Duke Cosimo II, but in 1637 Ferdinando I sold it to the marchesi Niccolini. Since then the building has remained unchanged and, over the years, with its fortress origins forgotten and its fabric untouched by any disfiguring alterations, it has taken on the appearance of a princely villa. The bleakness of some of its rooms has been alleviated by the addition of frescoes and the soldiers' quarters have been converted

Opposite: A large arch creates two linking areas. In days gone by this was the place where the servants would gather for brief moments of relaxation, but today the marchesi use it as a breakfast room. The austere, carefully chosen decor creates a rustic mood in perfect keeping with the room's rugged wooden ceiling and its ancient brick floor. Just a few items of furniture are enough to give the room that modest, workmanlike quality so characteristic of Tuscan interiors: a table, two benches and a simple cupboard, together with a few consciously decorative touches, such as the range of copper jugs.

Above: This is one of the many busts used to fine decorative effect throughout the garden.

Right: Each of the four corners of the villa proudly boasts original coats of arms belonging to the noble Florentine family of the Niccolini, two of them commemorating Corsi Salviati marriages

Below: This detail of the entrance staircase highlights the effective design of the balusters, that creates a pleasing interplay of geometrical shapes. The staircase was added during the eighteenth century, when the Medici building lost its rough quality and became the elegant villa that we see today: a villa that Lorenzo Niccolini and his wife, Alessandra Marcello, have preserved with a rare degree of affection and sensitivity. It is their belief that the house should be maintained in its centuries-old splendour, a task that involves conspicuous expense and a great deal of effort.

into rooms for the villa's farming business. All in all, the Niccolini family have for generations lived in an atmosphere of peace and serenity.

A majestic ceremonial staircase leads up to the villa's entrance, which takes the form of a vestibule very similar to a *ravelin*, a sort of projecting covered space that stood in front of the walls of fortresses. This vestibule, which has been made less gloomy over the years, is now lit by three large windows and is decorated in pale colours with the fantastic figures so beloved of late-eighteenth-century taste. The very elegant *salotto* borders on perfection. It is a warm mosaic of colours, with the brown of an early-nineteenth-century chest of drawers (whose handles are in the shape of satyr's heads), a writing table of the same period, and a marble mantelpiece bearing a bust of one of the marchese Lorenzo's ancestors. The walls are covered with trompe l'oeil views of an idealized landscape framed by the slender columns of a loggia that looks out over the distant panorama of towers, churches, lakes, rolling hills and green expanses. The whole scene, possibly by an English artist of the last century, is painted with a love of detail that carries it beyond reality into the realms of the imagination.

On entering the villa one catches a glimpse of a dimly lit fine piano and a large window, a dramatic effect seen down the long corridor leading to the ballroom.

The piano, on which stand old photographs of family members, is illuminated by the reflected light from the window which overlooks the garden.

The walls are enlivened by pleasantly decorative frescoes. But the finely executed fresco on the ceiling is a true work of art. Signed by the seventeenth-century painter Angelo Michele Colonna, it is a dynamic representation of a soldier being

Above: The coat of arms of the marchesi Niccolini, an argent lion rampant on an azure field with red bend. In 1452 a label with four pendants divided by the fleur-de-lis of Anjou was added.

Left: After crossing the threshold, visitors enter this impressive vestibule with its elegantly decorated vaulted ceiling. This room, the result of alterations carried out during the seventeenth and eighteenth centuries, originally possessed the characteristics of a *ravelin*, a structure once erected in front of the walls of fortresses.

Opposite: The *salotto* has the warmest decor in the villa. The most striking feature is the large trompe l'oeil loggia looking out over a sweeping landscape fresco which makes the room seem much larger than it is. Dating from the nineteenth century, it is thought to be the work of an English artist, as would seem to be confirmed by the landscape, which contains elements of the Tuscan countryside interpreted in a very English way.

carried up to heaven by a joyful throng of angels and putti.

The spacious dining room has a finely carved coffered ceiling, but its most impressive feature is its fireplace, a real *coup de théâtre* containing so many architectural allusions that it seems almost like a preparatory sketch for the facade of some sacred building. The mantelpiece is carved with the Latin word *Semper*, the motto of the Niccolini family, an encouragement never to give up, to remain steadfast in the face of adversity and not to be overwhelmed by life's difficulties.

This room looks out over the entire garden – bounded at one end by clipped box hedges interspersed with decorative busts – and beyond, to where the vast estate begins. This area of 570 hectares, half of which is under cultivation, is also a very

Above: No country villa with such deep-rooted traditions could be without its gun room. It is here that the Niccolini family, who have always been expert huntsmen, proudly display their trophies.

Opposite: The ceiling of the ballroom is embellished with this perspective fresco that reflects the aristocratic mood of the villa. A work of considerable artistic importance, it was painted during the seventeenth century by Angelo Michele Colonna.

Left: The monumental stone fireplace in the dining room, which dates from the eighteenth century, is still in perfect working order. Its figurative composition makes it a unique piece.

fine wildlife and game reserve.

But the creature that most epitomizes the Camugliano estate, even here, among the rustling trees and rolling meadows, is still the pheasant. The marchese is an enthusiastic breeder of these noble birds, which are found scattered throughout the grounds of the villa, often wandering in groups that provide a gently moving splash of colour.

VILLA L'APPARITA

Twenty-six iron-frame benches overlook a circular lawn framed by five plinths, each topped by a classical urn, while a rustic hedge encloses a green stage; in the distance lie the pastel shades of the fertile countryside and the elegant red-turretted outline of Siena. We are looking at a small open-air theater, born of the rational mind of a famous architect and conceived at the behest of a man with a burning passion for culture. This aesthete and Renaissance figure was fired by a single dream: to create a piece of Paradise, an idealized place apart, with the specific aim of pleasing the senses. The architect was the late Pietro Porcinai who was also commissioned to create a new layout for the Valley of the Kings and the Beaubourg gardens in Paris; the owner is Don Giovanni Guiso, a famous Sienese notary.

The theater hosts frequent musical performances and poetry readings aimed at glorifying the countryside and the gardens, an oasis of silence and privilege. But this is just one element in a stage set composed of lawns decorated with lavender bushes, broom, pomegranate and arbutus trees, with cypresses running down the side of a small hill on which stands a historic villa. The building is

Above: "All time not spent in loving is lost," reads the quotation from Torquato Tasso that Don Nanni Guiso has had fixed to a low wall in the vast garden surrounding his villa. It is also the philosophy of a man who sees existence in positive, dynamic terms.

Opposite: One of the rarest miniature theaters in the owner's extensive collection is this nineteenth-century piece of Italian manufacture. It was carved entirely by hand and decorated with a finesse and attention to detail that would be the envy of any great theater.

Overleaf: A ploughed field, a scattered flock of sheep, and a narrow cypress-fringed lane cutting across the countryside: elements in a quiet world where life is lived at a leisurely pace.

both a villa in the form of a farmhouse and also a sophisticated country house in the form of a villa.

This is the Villa l'Apparita, a strange and highly unique villa that even today leaves many questions unanswered. When Don Giovanni Guiso first came across it, it was in a pitiful state, its noble facade crumbling, its interior abandoned and decaying, its grounds completely neglected and uncultivated. But beneath this shabby appearance the notary's perceptive eye was able to detect something absolutely unique, something that excited his sensibilities as a theatrical enthusiast. That facade – with its two tiers of porticoes forming a double loggia that seemed almost suspended in the air, separate from the main body of the building – fired his curiosity, reminding him of a theater setting. It was the home for which he was searching.

He bought it and had it sympathetically restored, always respecting the original fabric. From then on he poured his soul into l'Apparita, which gradually began to yield up its secrets. Shortly afterwards, careful research revealed that the designer of the facade had been Baldassarre Peruzzi, a sixteenth-century

Above: Two views of the facade, which is probably the work of the great sixteenth-century Sienese architect Baldassarre Peruzzi, who created many major monuments in the countryside around Siena and also in Rome. The main building was added later and the facade, with its two superimposed porticoes forming a double loggia, was probably conceived as an elegant setting for parties and receptions in the midst of the lush countryside.

Right: Don Guiso's passion for the theater and performances is made immediately apparent by this small open-air stage. During the summer months poetry readings are held in this unusual setting, which has been designed along the lines of a Roman amphitheater.

Sienese architect, examples of whose genius can be seen in Tuscany and Rome. He also discovered what seems to be the likeliest hypothesis, namely that the facade was originally built without the main building, as a sort of picturesque folly to act as a backdrop for parties and receptions. But tastes change and the realities of life often lead to less poetic and certainly more functional solutions, which is how the farmhouse came to be added to the facade.

An arch of ivy frames the entrance, while the *salone* unfolds beneath four arches radiating out from a single pillar. It is an airy room with a strong sense of space, ideal for entertaining. The brick floor forms a warm, monochrome mosaic underfoot. A low, square table in a simple design with chamfered corners supports piles of books ranged around a vase of flowers. On the far wall a fine seventeenth-century blanket chest is the home of two candle holders in the shape of angels (now removed for restoration), who seem to shy away from the gaze of the visitor.

The small dining room has a monastic simplicity, a natural elegance. It contains a refectory table with a fruit-filled alabaster basket from Volterra, a tiny fifteenth-century Sardinian commode and nothing more. But anything more would be superfluous.

The first floor, on the other hand, represents Don Giovanni Guiso's

Opposite: The first room to greet the visitor is this *salone*, whose sweeping arches radiate from a single pillar. The light entering through the doors and windows creates a feeling of gentle warmth. The room picks up the aesthetic principles of the facade, and it is these that are most striking despite the equally enchanting taste of the furnishings.

Right: In the same room the eye of the visitor is drawn to this beautiful seventeenth-century blanket chest, on which stand two candlesticks in the form of angels (now undergoing restoration). These two carved wooden figures of the late seventeenth century, probably of the Roman school, once held candles to light a church altar, but now their spiritual and aesthetic power plays a purely decorative role.

childhood dream. Its rooms, which are dictated by his love of theater, lead off a long corridor punctuated by six wooden pillars with Corinthian capitals. There are many of these rooms, and their doors directly opposite each other create a cloister-like feeling.

But there are two Giovanni Guisos, and this is where his lively, intelligent and playful spirit reveals itself to his guests in its truest and least expected colours. There is the respected professional, and then there is the collector of dreams who roams the world, visiting antique stores and junk shops in search of miniature theaters for his famous collection, which has been written up in magazines and journals throughout the world. Puppet theaters of every nationality and every size range from quite large ones from the Brianza area in Lombardy, once used for open-air performances, to smaller ones from Austria, Romagna and Rome, to a series of German theater curtains, authentic examples of the genre. But the most fascinating items are the stage sets with scenes from major lyric operas that have been reproduced by Guiso himself after patient and painstaking research. There is one, built entirely in the Empire style, with a chest of drawers that fits into the palm of the hand and a perfect reproduction of a sofa on the same scale. There are also such period fittings as an English silver fruit bowl and a dressing-table set. Scenes have been reproduced from *Manon, Madame Butterfly* and *Il Trovatore*, to name but a few, and they have been set up with the invaluable assistance of such illustrious friends as Peter Hall, Raffaele del Savio, who is chief set designer of Florence's *Teatro Comunale*, and Luigi Baroni, Luchino Visconti's favourite lighting expert.

Guiso's miniature theaters have their own special day. In a room opening on to the loggia – where a statue of Bacchus, still endowed with the slimness of youth,

lifts his glass in a gesture of goodwill – Guiso's closest friends gather every New Year's Day to enjoy a unique spectacle. Don Giovanni Guiso disappears into a small booth at the back of the miniature theater set up for the performance. As darkness descends on the room, he starts up the record player and the air is filled with the opening notes of *Butterfly*, *Tosca*, the *Magic Flute* or *Othello*, every year a different opera. When the over-ture is finished, the curtain rises amid a mood of great solemnity. The slender puppets bring the show to life, skilfully manipulated by their owner.

At twilight, when the curtain falls, everything fades slowly into the shadows.

Above: Two more of the delightful miniature theaters from the collection. The top one, representing a middle-class drawing room, is early twentieth-century Emilian and made of precious wood and brass. The other, an Austrian piece from the last century, depicts a scene from Puccini's *Manon* and contains very rare examples of miniature period furniture and decorative items.

Opposite: Another view of the *salone*.

Right: One of the guest rooms, with walls painted by Maro Gorki Spender.

VILLA LA VAGNOLA

It is hard to concentrate on anything for long here: the senses are assailed from every direction. There is not a single empty space, nor a corner that has not been decorated with an attention to aesthetic detail that captures the visitor's attention with a hypnotic series of unique, beautiful objects: sofas, chairs, majolica and an endless variety of period pieces. There are clear echoes of cinema sets, and even more so of theater scenes. The first impression is one of admiration, but also of vague unease: it cannot be easy living amid such opulence. But then one soon realizes that all this is the result of an intellectual and aesthetic exercise that never degenerates into pomposity, and one feels slowly enveloped in an aura of warmth. The opulence, where it exists, is appropriate if not vital for the successful achievement of the desired effect: to create something unique, to progress beyond the banal, and to strive for a sense of inspired decorative freedom.

The men responsible for all this are the architect Enzo Mongiardino and the owner of the villa, Giancarlo Giammetti, president and deputy manager of the Valentino fashion company, Valentino Garavani S.p.A., as well as associate for

Above: A glimpse of the garden of Villa la Vagnola, a hidden, private world on the edge of the piazza in the ancient town of Cetona.

Opposite: A great wrought-iron gate reveals a small garden of geometric lawns adorned with large pots of orange and lemon trees. It is a place of contrasts, with areas of green alternating with open spaces. The garden, like the villa, bears a designer's signature. It was recently laid out by Paolo Peirone, renowned throughout the country for his splendid gardens in the Italian style reinterpreted in a modern vernacular. The surrounding area also contains some twenty Etruscan tombs.

almost thirty years of the famous designer himself. Mongiardino has contributed to the restoration of Villa la Vagnola by finding different solutions for every room, while the owner has brought his own special flair for colour to bear on the furnishings. The elegant garden, which is almost a continuation of the interior, has been created with the help of one of the most talented specialists in the field, the architect Paolo Peirone, who has succeeded in perfectly matching the mood of the villa.

The villa is not isolated in the middle of the countryside. In fact, one part of the building covers a large section of the Piazza Garibaldi at Cetona, an ancient and very historic town in the province of Siena. Although it is still in Tuscany, the Umbrian border is only a few miles away.

The name *la Vagnola* comes from the Tuscan habit of giving buildings nicknames derived either from their architectural characteristics, their location, or the name of the family that once owned them. It was in fact built in the sixteenth century for a noble family, the Terrosi-Vagnoli, who lived in it for many years. Conceived as an elegant residential showpiece, it also included a series of

Opposite: The interiors, by architect Enzo Mongiardino, reflect their designer's creative genius. This conservatory possesses a richly decorated ceiling, beneath which a wealth of disparate objects create an almost theatrical mood. In the foreground, a row of eighteenth-century figurines facing the window, flanked by two Meissen vases.

Below: An elegant corner of the same room.

Right: The villa has almost no internal doors, with the rooms leading one into another in an uninterrupted corridor. This particular corner contains a ceramic stove that perfectly reflects the eclectic nature of the villa's furnishings.

secondary structures of the sort found in other villas of the time; the lemon house and the Turkish pavilion that still stand in the grounds have now been adapted, the former into a gym and the latter into a place in which to relax after a swim in the nearby pool. The garden is a fine example of an Italian garden, whose graceful lines are a constant source of interest to visitors for whom the owner opens the grounds of the villa on the first Wednesday of every month. Two obelisks mark the entrance to this garden, which is lined with box hedges clipped into rectangular shapes, punctuated with perfectly trained large-leafed hedges that add a sense of movement.

The old stable, now transformed into an orangery, has a strangely monastic feel. With its large neo-Gothic windows, it could easily be taken for a religious building at first glance. Its interior is almost indescribable, filled as it is with so many precious objects and so many colours.

In designing certain decorative details, Mongiardino drew inspiration from a fine series of nineteenth-century watercolours depicting the interiors of large noble Austrian houses. These same watercolours now adorn one of the walls of the villa.

The conservatory, with its intricate ceiling decoration, is enclosed in Bohemian glass. Light tinged with blue and yellow floods into this stylish area used as a sitting room and filled with bright red sofas, an Empire-style armchair, a carpet that echoes the colours of the ceiling and a nineteenth-century canvas resting on an easel, although from a distance it seems to be suspended in midair between the armchair and a plant. Another area of the conservatory, which opens out on to the garden to the house, contains a touch of exoticism: on a small pile of books rests a row of valuable eighteenth-century figurines (*magots*) with moving heads, flanked by a pair of elegantly shaped Meissen vases. An unusual ceramic stove provides a particularly striking feature in one corner, where a daybed with floral cushions is set against green walls hung with small pictures. No provision has been made for doors, and the areas lead one into another in an almost dream-like sequence. A more classic touch is

Left: The spectacular library has a much more conventional quality, emphasizing the sober, ''cultural'' element. The other rooms make no attempt to stifle their natural exuberance; they demand our attention with their bright almost aggressive colours. The library, despite its size, projects a mood of much greater restraint. The bookcases lining the walls are in the Luccan style, while the large table in the center is of solid walnut.

Center: The reading area, which continues the mood of the library, contains an armchair and a large number of books in an elegant, glass-fronted bookcase.

Below: An antique painting and an eighteenth-century Meissen tureen.

Opposite: The ceiling carries on the decorative scheme created by Mongiardino, who was assisted in the villa's interior design by the owner himself, Giancarlo Giammetti. A close friend of the designer Valentino and also president of his company, Giammetti frequently took an active part in creating the colour schemes for his residence. In view of his close links with Valentino, it is interesting to note how the villa's colours contain echoes of the shades found in women's clothing.

provided by the library, which is inspired by Luccan examples and is decorated in the early-nineteenth-century style. At its center stands a fine oval table in walnut, piled with books and lit by a gold-painted lamp.

The decorative richness of the ceilings continues throughout the villa. Although they seem to be part of the original structure, the ceilings were in fact created in Mongiardino's own studio and then transferred to the villa. Another *salone* on the upper floor is crammed with objects: a gilt divan once owned by Princess Matilde, one of Napoleon's relatives, stands against a wall covered in an early-nineteenth-century French wallpaper with a motif of hangings and columns that mingle with the real columns, creating a visual interplay, an optical illusion that further enhances the feeling of fantasy. A mantelpiece supported by Egyptian figures links two beautiful bucolic paintings

Above: Straw hats are one of the owner's passions. These four examples hanging in the entrance hall look like something out of an advertisement.

Opposite: The first room in the villa, with its fascinating combination of Empire-style furniture and curious objects, is filled with surprises and gives a tantalizing taste of the villa's indefinable style.

Right: A detail of the conservatory that overlooks the old piazza in the small town of Cetona. Although the villa is in Siena, Umbria is only a short distance away, which is why the structure of certain rooms betrays Umbrian influences. The ceiling, which could easily be mistaken for an old one, is in fact another product of Mongiardino's fertile imagination.

Opposite: Another glimpse of the elegant conservatory, with an exotic statuette in the foreground.

Below: Here, in the old cellar, everything has been left as it used to be. Two sweeping arches arise from a single pillar, while two large windows create a feeling of gentle light and shade.

Right: The old Oriental-style pavilion was built in 1837 by the Terrosi-Vagnoli family for the visit of a pasha. It has now found a new role as a changing room for the swimming pool.

Below right: The facade of the old stables – whose strange appearance could easily be mistaken for a monastic building – is a product of the neo-Gothic taste so popular in the nineteenth century.

reminiscent of the work of Zurbarán.

It is the element of surprise that gives the villa its inimitable quality. Clearly designed to impress, it perfectly achieves its goal. A *salotto* like a picture gallery, a bedroom exploding with flowers, a canopied bed in the Empire style surrounded by extraordinary decorative richness, and on and on . . .

HOUSES & FARM-HOUSES

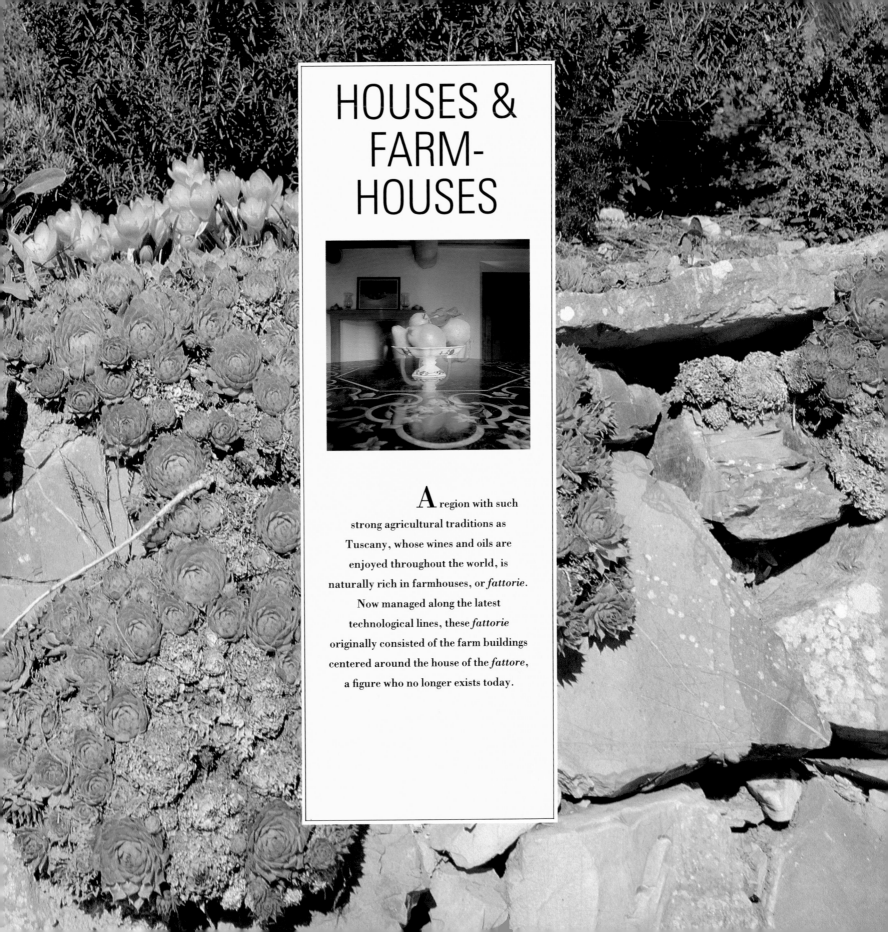

A region with such strong agricultural traditions as Tuscany, whose wines and oils are enjoyed throughout the world, is naturally rich in farmhouses, or *fattorie*. Now managed along the latest technological lines, these *fattorie* originally consisted of the farm buildings centered around the house of the *fattore*, a figure who no longer exists today.

CASA IL COLONELLO

A few stones surrounded by luxuriant vegetation whose strong roots were insinuating themselves into the rickety structure made up the ramshackle remains of an old, forgotten farmhouse hidden amid the dense green mosaic of the Luccan countryside. But, despite the fact that the building could claim no great architectural merit, it enjoyed a favoured, sun-drenched position. It seemed a crime to let these ruins, which had their own story to tell, be consigned to oblivion.

These were the thoughts that ran through the heads of Gregorio and Lilian Rossi di Montelera, who, using a great deal of imagination and maybe even pursuing some elusive childhood dream, saw this old, rustic house live again in their mind's eye.

They bought it, together with the surrounding land, and embarked on the work of restoration, assisted by the invaluable advice of an architect friend, Paolo Peirone. The work was carried out by Gregorio himself, helped by his brother Vittorio, both of whom spent long hours pondering how best to bring the old house back to life without altering its basic character. It had to revert to being a simple, rustic home, even if it was to be

Above: A "functional" work of art, this small iron table was created by Alberto Giacometti, perhaps to reproduce the serenity of an idyllic country scene.

Opposite: A large lawn takes up the grounds of the house. The luxuriant pergola, framed by pots of gardenias and azaleas, shades a table and chairs where the owners can relax in the open air, absorbed either in reading or in conversation with the many friends who frequently visit them, attracted not only by the pleasures of friendship but also by the atmosphere of reassuring tranquillity that envelops the house.

furnished with a luxury and intellectual consideration that it had never experienced before: the walls would remain the same and its shape would follow the old design. And this is how it has turned out. Today the house is much grander than before, but it still retains its attractive architecture of stout, reassuring walls, while the interior has a geometrical layout that reflects the functional requirements of a daily work routine rather than any aesthetic considerations.

A large, English-style lawn runs around the house, covering the small grassy mound that, from a distance, allows a perspective glimpse of the house and creates a great feeling of space. The stately, slender shapes of cypresses and the rustic, gnarled silhouettes of olive trees dot the land, sometimes individually and sometimes in small clusters.

The house is based on two elements of different height and very simple design. The entrance facade leads into a central *salone* filled with artistic references but decorated with incomparable simplicity: there is nothing forced here, nothing unnecessary. It is a harmonious balance of artwork, rugs, chairs and small tables, all sheltering beneath a pale ceiling that

Opposite: One of the many virtues of the airy central *salone* is its feeling of quiet, understated good taste. The pale colours of the walls, ceiling and furnishings were carefully chosen by the owner's wife and reflect her Brazilian origins. The room is remarkable for the way in which no one piece of furniture nor work of art dominates the others. Everything combines to create a feeling of careful harmony, from the pale yellow sofas and armchairs to the beautiful, early-twentieth-century Portuguese carpet.

Right: Upon entering the house, the visitor is greeted by the sight of this delicate divan of eighteenth-century form, the first of many works of art that grace the interior.

Below: The fine beamed ceiling of the dining room is part of the original building. In the foreground is a fine *scagliola* table with matching chairs.

seems to reach down to the objects with a heavy, concave embrace. The room has been carefully planned by signora Lilian, a Brazilian by birth, to create a feeling of gentle tranquillity: the pale yellow sofas and armchair, the beautiful early-twentieth-century Portuguese carpet with a pattern of flowers and leaves scattered on a pale ground, the charming card table surrounded by early-twentieth-century chairs, two enchanting eighteenth-century consoles of the Luccan school, and a contemporary mantelpiece supporting a sculpture of a horse by Vito Tongiani, who was also responsible for the painting on the wall. There is also an element of pure, schematic modernity in a very fine metalwork table bearing the silhouette of a horse eating the leaves of a tree, with three dogs looking on. It is a brilliant invention of the great Giacometti.

Most of the furniture takes the form of

Tuscan period pieces, especially of the Luccan school, such as the small eighteenth-century divan in the hall and the compact commode in the guest bedroom. The only concession to non-Tuscan style is another commode, a fine example of the Genoese rococo, with decorative details highlighted in gold. It stands in the master bedroom, where the central feature is a canopied bed designed and created by the architect Christian Badim, a close friend of the owners. The master bedroom also contains a delightful sculpture of the head of a young girl, a work by the American Joseph Ehrardy. It is a portrait of Lilian, who, perhaps in an excessive display of modesty, professes not to like the work very much.

Above: The master bedroom also contains a striking sculpture of a young woman in profile. It is a splendid, almost girlish likeness of signora Lilian.

Left: Throughout the house the owners have favoured a Tuscan style of decor, a choice also reflected in the furniture made by famous Tuscan craftsmen, particularly those of the Lucchesia. An elegant exception to the rule, however, is this lively eighteenth-century dresser with its lacquered gold decoration; it is a Genoese piece and one of the most prized items in the house.

Opposite: This elegant modern canopied bed was created by architect Christian Badim, a friend of the conti Rossi di Montelera. Part of the beamed ceiling, which contributes greatly to the room's feeling of warmth, was rescued from the original fabric of the building.

Left: The feeling of elegant simplicity carries into the guest bedroom, which contains this fine painted dresser of the mid seventeenth century.

Opposite: Ploughed fields give way to mountain slopes. Although much of Tuscany is flat, it also contains areas of often inaccessible mountains.

Below: These two views give an idea of the spacious garden, with its green lawns and the gentle hill that conceals the Casa Il Colonello from prying eyes.

The house is known as Il Colonello because, when it was still a simple country home, it appears once to have belonged to a colonel in the Italian army. Steeped in memories, it is a place that today, thanks to that gamble taken on a forlorn pile of ruins, once again warms itself in the strong sun of a landscape in which ostentation has no place.

FATTORIA DELL'UGO

Rampant ivy clambers everywhere, spilling across the facade. The cloak of leaves and tendrils forms a living green fresco in the summer warmth, becoming tinged with a lazy, languid red in autumn as everything begins to turn slowly and inexorably to yellow.

Two buttress-like elements frame the facade of the Fattoria dell'Ugo, which overlooks a small park filled with tall trees, a rich natural habitat kept intentionally uncultivated by its present owners. A number of lemon trees set in large pots decorate the garden, most of which is laid to lawn, while an old well, itself swathed in ivy and adorned at the base with flower-filled pots, evokes a bygone age. The building, which has been extended over the years, is of late sixteenth-century appearance, with a number of later additions. Most likely the central tower was originally a hunting lodge and the structure was not transformed into a country residence until some time during the seventeenth or eighteenth century.

The Fattoria dell'Ugo, noted for its excellent wines, stands near San Casciano, a lively area on the fringes of where Chianti Classico is produced. The fat-

Above: The *salone*, a rather austere room, is enlivened by these putti bearing aloft a garland that encircles the bust of a woman. These decorative elements, clearly of eighteenth-century inspiration, are frequently found in houses of this sort. Like the Fattoria Dell'Ugo, such residences were originally hunting lodges or fortified strongholds, buildings of lesser architectural importance that were subsequently transformed into country retreats for use by noble families during the summer months.

Opposite: This bedroom is a room of exemplary elegance. The eighteenth-century canopied bed reaches toward the ornate ceiling, which is covered in frescoes evoking the lives of the peasants and the local lord.

toria has been in the Florentine family of the Amici Grossi for six generations. Franco and Giovanna Amici Grossi, business partners as well as brother and sister, spend their working days here and, during the summer, also live here with their respective families. The fattoria is a link with a carefree past, not only where they work, but also a place they played together as children, a place with which they have both had an enduring love affair. Franco Amici Grossi felt unfulfilled working in a bank in Florence, while the estate, which was not under full-time supervision, faced two choices: either it was completely overhauled or it ran the risk of coming to an unhappy end. It was these considerations that made him decide to devote all his efforts to wine making and to the expansion and promotion of the business. When his sister followed his example it was rather like a return to their past.

In the early days life was not easy, as all the infrastructure needed to be completely renovated. The Amici Grossi did not lose heart, however; they approached the work with enthusiasm, reviving the fortunes of the enterprise and restoring its competitiveness. The result is that

Opposite: The *salone* is a room of geometrics. The coffered ceiling is richly painted, while the walls display a number of antique prints, some of which portray members of the Medici family. Three eighteenth-century female busts stand above the doors, which are framed by small trompe l'oeil Doric columns.

Right: The atrium links the front door with the *salone*. Its vault has a seventeenth-century decoration of symbolic and allegorical figures: the god Pan chasing a girl, Bacchus's chariot drawn by mythical animals, and figures of young women symbolizing the four seasons.

Overleaf: A delicate carpet of flowering irises covers a broad sweep of land.

Below: This lunette bears a curious painting by an unknown artist, almost certainly the same artist responsible for the atrium frescoes. He has portrayed his own likeness on the right, but his place at the easel has been taken by the figure of a monkey wielding a brush. This may be a display of modesty, or perhaps a gesture of ridicule.

today the two of them are owners of a splendid complex, with an estate producing wines of the highest quality.

The compact, rectangular entrance hall has a barrel-vaulted ceiling decorated with an elegant seventeenth-century fresco filled with figures: the god Pan chasing a young maiden, the chariot of Bacchus drawn by fantastic animals and personifications of the four seasons. There is also a self-portrait of the painter, next to a monkey seated at an easel: a sign of modesty, or perhaps a provocative reaction to the owners not having paid him enough?

The *salone* is spacious, albeit austere. The seventeenth-century Tuscan bookcase is adorned with small antique prints, while the walls are decorated with prints of the Medici family, forming a portrait gallery of the grand ducal family. Each of the three doors leading off the *salone* is

surmounted by a fresco of two chubby winged putti holding a garland of flowers around a female head, a decorative conceit of clearly rococo inspiration. A gallery of grotesques gazes down from the fine wooden ceiling. These faces of satyrs, gods and wizards, sometimes comical and sometimes sinister, are probably the work of the same painter responsible for the entrance hall fresco, who may have been a pupil of Poccetti and thus an artist of the early-seventeenth-century Florentine school. It resembles the sort of fanciful, satirical work favoured by a school of fresco artists active in Tuscany at the time. The ceiling of a small adjoining room is decorated – by a much less expert hand – with scenes of agricultural work: the *vendemmia*, the harvest, and the sowing of the seed.

A *salotto*, with canvases depicting the feats of various ancestors, leads into a

Above and right: Almost every room in the Fattoria dell'Ugo is decorated with naturalistic, sometimes grotesque motifs. The ceiling of the *salotto* displays the fresco to the right, whose central tondo contains a hunting scene further attesting to the building's original function.

Opposite: Every corner of the fattoria's kitchen radiates a typically Tuscan feeling: the functional fireplace, the informal table and the interesting set of shelves, probably dating from the seventeenth century, that holds a number of dishes and pieces of seventeenth-century Florentine majolica. This room, which has remained virtually unchanged for six generations, is where the two branches of the Amici Grossi family gather every mealtime, especially during the summer, to enjoy a true culinary feast. They eat only Tuscan-style food: a simple yet sophisticated diet of meat grilled over charcoal, copious vegetables, and excellent desserts, all accompanied by the estate's own wine. This choice is in itself a reflection of the Amici Grossi's love and respect for the fattoria and for their native Tuscany.

large, typically Tuscan kitchen. The magnificent seventeenth-century cupboard, which is actually a piece of stone furniture embedded in the wall, displays beautiful seventeenth-century Florentine majolica dinner and soup plates.

A long corridor with many rooms off it leads to a particularly elegant bedroom featuring an outstanding antique canopied bed crowned by a carved wooden cornice with gilt borders. The ceiling has a narrative theme, with scenes of hunting (probably a reference to the building's original role) and fishing, vignettes depicting the life and people of the countryside and figures of noble lords, who, with their rich dress and proud poses, contrast starkly with the peasants shown going about their work. The ceiling is also dotted with allegorical figures: putti on horseback, deer and fantastic female figures. The wall decorations, which date to the second half of the eighteenth century, depict views of classical ruins.

The Fattoria dell'Ugo is a place of many moods. There is the elegance of its paintings, the austerity of its rooms, the romance of its facade and garden, but there are also its wine-making activities, which make it a living organism rather than a museum. It is this feeling of being isolated yet lived in that gives it its special quality. The owners' only source of regret is that the fattoria lies a mere two miles outside the area whose wines have the

right to call themselves "Chianti Classico." The soil is to all intents and purposes the same, but boundaries are boundaries and so the wines bearing the Fattoria dell'Ugo label, which are renowned for their quality, cannot bear the world-famous *galletto nero* (black rooster) seal. Since the brother-and-sister partnership has devoted itself full-time to the fattoria, the reputation of its wines has grown in leaps and bounds. An average of 660,000 pounds of grapes is now gathered each season, almost all of which is turned into wine for sale both in Italy and abroad. Red wines, a particular speciality here, are made, as the label proclaims, with Sangiovese and Cabernet Sauvignon grapes.

A great deal of care is also taken with the manufacture of extra-virgin olive oil, although, despite incessant demand, production has had to be drastically curbed as a result of the cold weather that struck Tuscany in 1985 killing large numbers of olive trees. But Franco and Giovanna Amici Grossi have not given up. Today the countless olive trees damaged by the frost are springing back to life so that soon the precious oil from the farm will once again whet the appetites of those for whom a region's cooking reflects the culture of its inhabitants. In this respect, as in many others, the people of Tuscany, who favour simple yet excellent food, are among the most cultured.

Above: A detail of the monumental fireplace in the kitchen.

Opposite: The facade is divided by two elements projecting into the garden, while the ivy insinuates itself relentlessly into every corner of the building. The late-sixteenth-century structure began life on a much smaller scale as a hunting lodge and was transformed during the seventeenth century into a rustic yet elegant building.

Below: The ivy entwined around the old well strikes a romantic note in this corner of the garden.

CASA IL CASTELLARE

A letter penned by the Swiss writer Denise de Uthemann to the present owners of Il Castellare struck a note of warning. In eloquent and impassioned tones, she stressed the necessity of respecting the colours of the countryside when redoing the interiors. Only this way could they possibly achieve a successful balance between the rooms in the house and their natural surroundings.

Paolo Panerai, a well-known journalist, and his wife, Fioretta, who oversees the estate's small but highly professional vine-growing and wine-producing business, were both convinced this heartfelt advice was absolutely right since, as the previous owner, Denise de Uthemann had already put her theory into practise and decorated the house with extraordinary sensitivity. The Panerais began immediately by carefully furnishing the interiors with Tuscan pieces whose colours would reflect the Chianti countryside.

The simple, elegant shape of the Castellare estate stands at the center of a mosaic of cypresses, olive trees and vines, surrounded by the unique palette of the Chianti countryside. The house was built using stones from a now-vanished monastery. The monks who once lived here

Above: Every Tuscan farmhouse has its devotional image, generally carved out of stone or modelled in clay by local craftsmen.

Opposite: A view of the highly original architecture of Il Castellare, which was built entirely out of the stones of an old monastery. Its owners not only like to relax here in the peaceful Chianti countryside, but also to work. The house is linked to a highly productive vine-growing and wine-making enterprise. The wine produced by the Panerai, which bears the "I Sodi di San Niccolò" label, is a Chianti Classico. It is made exclusively from grapes grown in these vineyards, on which great care is lavished, particularly by signora Fioretta, who divides her time between Milan and her beautiful home in Chianti.

had also devoted much time to tending their vines. The same stones were used to build the low walls that terrace the grounds, and it is this rugged material that gives the building its reassuringly solid appearance and imbues it with such a timeless quality. Although Paolo and Fioretta Panerai are both from Milan, they are now fully immersed in the Tuscan way of life, which they have embraced with unaffected simplicity. Like Il Castellare, they too now blend in with their surroundings.

Beyond, a garden of lawns, the dense greenery of a few cypresses, a small patch of rosemary, countless native plants, and isolated rows of vines lead into the vineyards that stretch out across the fields. The small swimming pool has been fitted unobtrusively into a flat area, again paved with stones from the old monastery.

The rooms have been left untouched as far as possible, with no attempt to introduce elements of "urban" or modern decor. The advice, almost the earnest wish, of the Swiss writer has been respected and the interior constantly echoes the colours of the countryside. On the ground floor there is a typically Tuscan

Below: The house stands behind a small wall and is surrounded by the luxuriant green foliage of its cypresses. This view of Il Castellare shows the front of the building. In the lower photograph, the entrance can be clearly seen, sheltering beneath a tiled porch covered in climbing plants. The warm, honey-coloured stone of the house is reflected in the sitting room curtains and repeated throughout the house.

kitchen and a small interconnecting dining room and sitting room. The rustic brick floor gives the kitchen a very warm feeling, while the fine wooden mantelpiece frames a display of old beaten-copper utensils. There are also wine bottles, chosen for their decorative qualities; a large basket of fruit, reminiscent of a still life; sausages hung up to mature; and jars of homemade preserves, prepared according to traditional local recipes.

The spacious sitting room, lit by French windows in brick arches, is divided into different areas linked by a common decorative theme. A charming fireplace with a brick hearth stands at the far end, while three sofas, upholstered in a handwoven Tuscan fabric and grouped around a refectory-style coffee table, create a secluded seating area. The burnt gold of the carpet, woven in the Maremma region, is echoed in the curtains, which were

Opposite: A glimpse of the kitchen, which is typically Tuscan in style; its central feature is a rustic brick fireplace framed by an attractive display of beaten copper utensils. The figs in the basket were gathered from trees in the garden.

Left: The spacious sitting room is divided in two by a small brick arch. Light floods in through arch-framed windows, which provide a direct link with the garden just a few steps away. An exclusively Tuscan decorative theme runs through the sitting room, starting with the carpet, which was made in the Maremma region, and continuing through the sofas that are covered in a hand-woven Tuscan fabric, and the curtains, made by master craftsmen in Florence.

Below: This elegant chair forms part of the sparse yet carefully chosen furnishings, which consist of seventeenth- and nineteenth-century Tuscan pieces.

also made by local craftsmen. The floor of the dining room is covered with rush matting in a gentle departure from the Tuscan mood, while the dominant colour scheme is provided by the white upholstery and curtains, which are also handmade.

A niche in one wall contains a fine collection of Deruta plates and rare decanters whose elongated shapes resemble those of old apothecary jars. The bedrooms on the upper floor, which carry on the "local" theme, all possess wrought-iron beds, just like the ones found in old farmhouses. In the guest bedroom, whose ceiling of wooden beams gives it a strong rustic feel, a charming terra-cotta roundel of the Madonna and Child on one wall provides a simple and unassuming touch of spirituality.

The Panerai home contains such charmingly hospitable touches as the

Left: The mood of the sitting room is repeated in the dining room, where the emphasis is yet again on Tuscan materials. The fabric used for the chairs and the white curtains is the work of local craftsmen. The owners have decided to retain the beamed ceiling, a typical feature of this type of house. The only concession to a different style of decor is provided by the attractive rush matting.

Opposite: All the bedrooms in the house boast wrought-iron beds and beamed ceilings. In this, the guest bedroom, there is a splendid nineteenth-century bed and a terra-cotta tondo of the Virgin and Child.

Below: Connoisseurs will appreciate this fine collection of Deruta plates and decanters displayed in a niche in the wall. The elongated, transparent shapes of the decanters impart a feeling of elegance and fragility.

comfortable armchairs in the *salottino*, which precedes the entrance arch leading into the sitting room; other equally inviting chairs stand on the lawn directly opposite. Outside, the pleasure of the surroundings lies not within the furniture and decorative elements but in the unspoilt natural landscape that first cast its spell on the Panerai. They wanted a home in the Tuscan countryside and, in the process, they discovered not only the breathtaking delights of the Chianti region, but also this house, which the Swiss writer had put on the market. Considering the heartfelt advice she offered the new owners, she must still have had great affection for this house: a house built with love out of the stones of an old monastery, and designed for a simple, elegant life, in perfect keeping – both in side and out – with the mood of the Chianti countryside, a mood of light and silence.

CASA DI POGGIO AL POZZO

Perhaps this house ought not to be described or investigated in detail: any dissection, any minute examination, might diminish it, deprive it of its integrity. Ideally, Poggio al Pozzo should be experienced and "lived" in all its hospitable atmosphere and charm.

On entering the house for the first time, the visitor senses that everything is as it should be and that the poetic elegance of the interior is an accurate reflection of its owner's good taste. It is the "simple" home of an aesthete, who has endowed it with strong, painterly touches, using a range of pastel shades that recur in every room and seem to spill out into the surrounding countryside.

It is the home of the English artist Teddy Millington Drake, a man of great subtlety and sensitivity who spends his life immersed in colour; even the way in which he expresses himself reflects his activities as an artist. He is a cordial and courteous host whose manner betrays a certain underlying reserve.

The grounds of the house have a natural, "unplanned" quality combining elements inspired by the Italian garden with others reminiscent of the freer, more English style. The mosaic of hedges, low

Above: This view shows the Casa di Poggio al Pozzo set amid the hilly landscape of the Chianti countryside around Siena and surrounded by trees. It is a typical farmhouse with a broad, solid structure.

Opposite: The gardens surround the building in an almost circular shape. Teddy Millington Drake planned the garden, which he looks after himself, as a free interpretation of the conventional rules of garden layout, a symbol of his freedom and a place of constant change. He regards the house as a thing of great but firmly established beauty, whereas the garden is a more creative space where new elements can constantly be introduced.

walls, and paths is skilfully arranged in an uncontrived way. The garden is in perfect harmony with the surrounding countryside, whose colours it shares; countless shades of green splashed with a few brightly hued flowers.

The house is a fine building arranged on two floors, with a large arched terrace overlooking the luxuriant Chianti countryside and on the ground floor a broad, shady entrance. This entrance once housed the stables, but all that now remains are the bare walls, with a solid, rustic arch dividing the area in two. A beam of light enters through a window and floods over the room, creating an almost photographic effect. In the background, an unusual brass-studded Indian chest dating from the nineteenth century creates a fine decorative feature, while the walls are enlivened with highly imaginative chromatic effects painted by Millington Drake himself.

A few steps away, a small interconnecting room houses a collection of ceramics painted by the artist: a series of plates displaying an intriguing range of abstract patterns. At the top of a steep and narrow staircase that leads unobtrusively up to the first floor stands a delightful

Left: The facade of the house displays certain pretensions to grandeur in these two superimposed arches, one on each floor. Although originally a simple peasant dwelling, it was clearly more luxurious than the average house of this kind.

Below: The great arch supporting the upper floor shelters an area looking out on to the spacious terrace. It is used by the artist at mealtimes or to enjoy an afternoon cup of tea. The house provides Millington Drake with a great source of artistic creativity; it is here that he finds his richest vein of expressive freedom.

Opposite: A delightful gallery of plates, all painted by the artist, which echoes different colours in the house.

Below: This spacious entrance hall, originally the stables where the cattle were kept, is divided by a large arch. In the background stands a fine nineteenth-century Indian chest, while the random patterns on the wall, painted by the artist himself, enhance the intellectual mood of the room. A narrow staircase leads from here to the upper floor, where the large sitting room and the numerous bedrooms are located.

sort of pantry, fitted into a very small space, which seems to anticipate all the many other rooms leading off it. Everything needed by the perfect host is ranged along a low, brick wall: spirits, beer and soft drinks, along with snacks to accompany the guests' apéritifs.

The adjoining room, however, the sitting room with its high ceilings and tranquil atmosphere, is very much the focal point of the house. Only the sound of the

Opposite: A view of the most spectacular room in the house. This warm sitting room has been designed by the artist, who has furnished the entire house in his own inimitable and highly individual style. He has, however, respected and even emphasized the original features of the house: the sober, rustic fireplace, the lofty beamed ceiling, and the simple stairs leading up to an attic room that once served as a *piccionaia*, or pigeon loft. The room features a number of different areas: the fireplace, for example, acts as the focal point of an area for reading and relaxation, with sofas and a dramatic daybed.

Below and right: At the top of the stairs leading up to the first floor, before entering the sitting room guests encounter this small room that acts as a sort of pantry in which they can help themselves to a pre-prandial drink. In the room is the original sink and a low wall with a brick top. The walls display a series of works by the artist.

wood crackling in the grate disturbs the peace. In bygone days this was a large country kitchen, where the women toiled at the stove as they waited for their menfolk to return from working in the fields. Now it is a welcoming room divided into three areas: one for reading, with armchairs, a sofa and a low, square table groaning under the weight of its books; another, centered on the fireplace, with sofas, a daybed and a large cushion reserved for Sandy, the artist's faithful dog; and, finally, one containing a table flanked by two fine eighteenth-century chairs covered in red fabric. Opposite, a low stone wall with a brick base supports a wooden head of Christ, another example of nineteenth-century Indian art. At the far end of the room a flight of wooden steps, part of the house's original fabric, leads up to the *piccionaia*. This space, in which the peasants used to raise pigeons, has been transformed into a light and airy library, whose walls are adorned with nine of the artist's own watercolours that represent a happy synthesis of descriptive grace and pale, harmonious colours.

Leading off the sitting room are a number of rooms that still retain their role as bedrooms. Reserved for guests, each one has its own muted colour scheme. There is the green room, whose fine bed is curtained in that colour; the red room; the pink room; and, finally, the owner's own bedroom, the white room.

A low building, just a stone's throw from the house and once the site of the old threshing floor, now houses Millington Drake's studio. A table is crammed with plans and sketches, while up a small flight of steps there is an extensive display of the artist's work. Paintings stand to attention, some finished, some awaiting completion. The room reverberates with the artist's creative energy, an energy that can be sensed not just here but in every corner of the property.

Above left: A canopied bed in one of the guest bedrooms, whose decor and fabrics display a strong linear quality.

Above: The wooden staircase in the sitting room leads up to this room, formerly the pigeon loft. The birds entered and left by the rectangular holes that dot the walls. It is an elegant room with a very intimate feel, containing a writing desk, two sofas, a bookcase and a series of the artist's own watercolours.

Left: The charming umbrella stand gives a clue to Millington Drake's Anglo-Saxon origins.

Opposite: The old threshing floor now houses the painter's studio. The many half-finished canvases and scattered paints are a reflection of Millington Drake's creative energies.

FATTORIA DI FONTERUTOLI

A splash of red-roofed houses nestles in a lush green valley, a serenity undisturbed by noise. At Fonterutoli, an ancient village near Castellina in Chianti, silence rules. Though they are very hospitable people, its few inhabitants do not believe in wasting their words.

Beyond a large, wrought-iron gate stands the elegant, villa-like home of the marchese Lapo Mazzei, president of a notable Florentine finance house and also of the Consorzio del Chianti Classico, whose members include most of the wine producers of this region, where wine is a passion and a way of life.

Many of the buildings at Fonterutoli have belonged to this ancient Florentine family since 1435, when a young damsel, Madonna Smeralda dei Mazzei, came to live here as wife of the local lord, Piero di Agnolo da Fonterutoli. The site had already been inhabited for several centuries, and it is even believed that there was an Etrusco-Roman settlement in the area, a theory supported by the discovery of a number of tombs and also by its name. Fonterutoli is derived from the Latin place name *Fons Rutuli* which means origin of the Rutoli, an ancient people of Latium. During the late Middle Ages the

Above: This simple eighteenth-century niche is one of the first sights to greet visitors entering the house.

Opposite: With the small town of Fonterutoli behind us, wrought-iron gates open to reveal the elegantly secluded home of the marchesi Mazzei. The facade of unfinished stone, which recalls earlier, rougher days, has been softened by later additions. The *loggetta* was built on to the corner and overlooks a small, elegant garden of clipped hedges leading to the small park and the swimming pool. The courtyard is adorned with large terra-cotta pots containing lemon trees, an almost indispensible feature of Tuscan houses.

town, which was clustered around the walls of a castle, must have enjoyed a certain importance; in 1201 and 1208, delegations arrived both from Florence and Siena to discuss peace treaties and to establish the exact boundaries of the areas that each of them would administer.

But almost nothing remains at Fonterutoli of these distant times. The medieval buildings were destroyed on several occasions by Sienese raiders, hence the attractive buildings that now greet the visitor date from the fifteenth century or later. There are some sixteenth- and seventeenth-century houses, however, that were built on the medieval remains, and in some of these, fragments of much earlier walls can still be seen incorporated into the structure, a feature that further contributes to Fonterutoli's evocative sense of history.

The Mazzei villa was itself built during the reconstruction of Fonterutoli, although there are also much later additions, such as the small loggia overlooking the garden erected in the early 1900s in a vaguely Renaissance style. Externally the building has a strongly organic shape, with structural walls that

Right and far right: These two views of the house, from the courtyard and from the garden, show the exact layout of the Mazzei house, which takes the form of two blocks linked by the elegant *loggetta* with its three columns.

Below: A fine arch of rusticated stone adorns the front entrance, which is crowned by the coat of arms of the Mazzei. Over the years, members of this ancient Florentine family – which has played a prominent part in public life since the fifteenth century – have distinguished themselves in a variety of different fields.

are made of rough, unworked stone.

The door, framed by a delightful arch of rusticated stone, affords access to the elegant, antique-filled entrance hall. Two eighteenth-century chests of similar design stand opposite each other; two small canvases depict the heads of saints; an eighteenth-century niche displays ornaments; and an umbrella stand holds walking sticks that belonged to ancestors of the owners.

The room adjoining the entrance hall acts as Lapo Mazzei's study. Embodying the marchese's two great loves – books and horses – this room projects a feeling of well-ordered activity, the table strewn with books and papers, pens and notebooks. An Empire bookcase with slender black columns contains a valuable collection of works published during the seventeenth, eighteenth and nineteenth centuries, with a few others of even earlier date. The family documents,

Below: This attractive grouping of objects has all the qualities of a painting. An eighteenth-century chest supports a vase of flowers picked in the garden by the marchesa, while, in a gesture of ancient symmetry, the Mazzei coat of arms is flanked by two seventeenth- or possibly eighteenth-century canvases depicting the heads of saints. The coat of arms, composed of three gold maces on a red ground, attests to the family's membership of the guild of armourers. The collection of umbrellas, whips and walking sticks is just one of the many indications of the English nature of the owners, who are, among other things, great horse enthusiasts.

Right: The kitchen of the Fattoria di Fonterutoli, a classic of its kind, contains such traditional elements as a nineteenth-century kitchen cupboard and a fine marble-topped table that provides a focal point similar to that found in old farmhouses. The marchesa takes particular care of this room: she believes that the kitchen should be accorded the same degree of attention as that paid to other rooms. Despite the fact that it is used several times each day, it is always as immaculate as any other part of the house.

ancient scientific treatises and historical and philosophical texts all remain in their original bindings of a warm, evocative parchment colour. The owner's love of horses is clearly evident here, with every sort of riding equipment displayed on the walls and spilling on to a small side table: riding hats, whips, bits and saddlebags. There is even a hat like the ones worn by the *butteri*, the Tuscan cowboys who tend the local herds. Another striking feature of the study is its fine fireplace, which was incorporated into the building during the early decades of the century by the grandfather of the present marchese.

The signora Carla Mazzei is the gracious and hardworking mistress of the house at Fonterutoli. While taking her regular walks around the property she is never surprised to be greeted by a galloping horse, almost a thoroughbred, high in the withers, with expressive eyes and perfect stance. It is the mount of the

Opposite: This is the entrance hall, with the door on the right leading into the study. The staircase is the work of the same architect who designed the *loggetta* at the end of the nineteenth century.

Right: The marchese Mazzei's study houses this extensive library containing a collection of very valuable books, printed during the seventeenth, eighteenth and nineteenth centuries, many still with their original bindings. They are mainly documents dealing with the legal and economic affairs of the Grand Duchy of Tuscany, although some of them are classical texts. The room also contains the family archive, dating back to the fourteenth century. The armchair is used by the marchese for reading amid the unbroken silence of this great house.

Below: The book collection was begun by the ancestors of the present owners, who have extended it and turned it into a sort of family tradition; these books are some of the finest in the collection.

marchese, who rides away into the rolling countryside to escape the tensions, the stress and the strain of his very active life.

A small stone staircase of the nineteenth century leads to the upper floor, providing access to the *loggetta*, which was designed by the same architect. On the upper floor there is a spacious dining room decorated with a splendid panelled ceiling. Above the great fireplace is a fine display of old majolica bearing the family coat of arms. Two large canvases, more interesting for the fact that they portray two members of the Medici dynasty than for their artistic merit, grace the walls. Also in the dining room hangs the genealogical chart of the great Florentine family, a large canvas with an idealized Tuscan landscape in the background. The labyrinthine branches of this great tree contain the names of all the Mazzei, from the first, a certain Giunta, to Arrigo, Filippo, Lapo, Donato, Simone and Arrigo. The same names often recur, many of them belonging to such notable figures as bishops, statesmen and ambassadors. This family tree stops in the seventeenth century, but the names continue in another one, located in a second room; although less interesting and picturesque, the chart is nevertheless equally important for the history of the family. The final names here are Filippo, Francesco and Jacopo, who, as the three sons of the marchesi Lapo and Carla, are the last scions of this noble house. Soon the names of their children will in turn be added to the list, as history lives on.

A painting in an adjacent *salotto* depicts a gentle-faced Madonna tenderly cradling the infant Jesus. It is part of a fresco and has thus been tentatively attributed to the late Mannerist painter

Left and above: Another view of the study, dominated by its books and given a monumental quality by the fine old fireplace, which originally graced another remote residence in the region and was brought here by the marchese's grandfather during the 1920s. In the background to the left (and shown above) is a corner filled with riding hats, whips and saddlebags that reflect the owners' love of horses. Every day, without fail, Lapo Mazzei goes for a long gallop through the hills of the surrounding countryside. It is his way of relaxing from the tensions of a working life that finds him involved in so many different activities.

Opposite: The dining room, with its massive wooden ceiling, continues the mood of the house, although perhaps here there is a feeling of greater austerity. The large painting displays the genealogy of the family, with a rustic landscape inspired, naturally enough, by the Tuscan countryside. The tree bears the names of countless ancestors stretching back to the seventeenth century. It is a record of men and women now long forgotten, whose memorial lies in this canvas and in the buildings of Fonterutoli.

Bernardino Poccetti, whose works adorn the walls of so many Florentine churches and palazzos. An elegant occasional table displays a variety of small personal objects, including silver snuffboxes, a tiny eye glass and a magnifying glass several centuries old.

The *loggetta* looks out over the garden and the park that lies beyond. The small hanging garden is an elegant area of box hedges laid out in irregular patterns, with other hedges to the side marking the boundary of the small park. At the edge of the park an elegant gravel pathway leads through flowerbeds and lemon trees, shaded by rows of cypresses.

The memory of Marianna Tommasi Aliotti, the marchese Lapo's grandmother, lives on in the design of these grounds. There was no need for an expert designer: all it took was this lady's enthusiasm to ensure that the austere and rugged Fattoria di Fonterutoli was embellished with an Italian garden and a small, romantic park in the English style. Her reward has been the admiration with which she is still remembered by her grandchildren and great-grandchildren.

Outside the house stand the cellars, shrouded in silence, a silence that symbolizes the secretive life of this cluster of buildings, so rich in memories. The cellars are in a state of constant ferment: not only in Italy, but throughout the world there is increasing demand for the

Above: This view of the garden shows the imaginative pattern of box hedges laid out by Marianna Tommasi Aliotti, the marchese's grandmother, who created this patch of green as her tribute to the Italian-style garden.

Opposite: The fittings in this room clearly proclaim its role as a bathroom, but without them it could easily be mistaken for some noble *salotto*.

Below: The small park lies to the right of this relaxing avenue of shrubs and flowers.

Chianti Classico produced here. This is only to be expected when one considers that the Mazzei family have been making wine since time immemorial. But it is not only a case of tradition: today, the family is directly involved in the running of the vineyard, a commitment to maintaining high standards which guarantees the special quality of its wines and ensures that they reflect the benefits of so many years' experience. The young Filippo Mazzei plays a particularly skilful and enthusiastic role in the affairs of the vineyard.

The vines, which lie between 350 and 550 meters above sea level (1150–1800 feet), stretch as far as the borders of Castellina and Radda in Chianti, over land containing a high percentage of sandstone and limestone that play a part in giving the wines their special bouquet. The total land area is 384 hectares (950 acres), but only 38 hectares (94 acres) are laid down to specialized vineyards.

The three brands of wine produced at Fonterutoli are appreciated by the most discerning palates, and the olive groves also produce an extremely sought-after olive oil. A well-known journalist, who writes for the *New York Times*, judged their extra-virgin olive oil one of the ten best oils in the world.

CASA IL PRATO

Certain decorative features in this house betray the English origins of its owners: the lace on the beds, the colours of the rooms, the Oriental touches, the carefully gauged, natural layout of the garden and the elegant verandah, with its feeling of easy comfort and relaxation. In other aspects, however, Il Prato is still a small, two-hundred-year-old Tuscan farmhouse, both in its architecture and its interiors, thanks to the owners' respect for tradition and to their careful selection of objects linked to local life.

Douglas and Judith Wilson bought the house some years ago, after they fell under the spell of the Tuscan countryside. The English have always had a special feeling for Tuscany because in it they find the same aesthetic climate as at home: the harmonious feeling of a landscape still respected by its inhabitants and an honest, well-ordered lifestyle. Il Prato is their holiday home, a place far from their native London, but it is a living house, ready to welcome them at any time of the year, like an old friend in whom one can confide in the certain knowledge of always being understood.

In the garden, the Wilsons have successfully met the challenge of packing

Above: Douglas and Judith Wilson's house stands in the heart of the Chianti countryside. Londoners born and bred, they fly to Pisa every summer, and occasionally at other times of the year, to spend time in their Tuscan home. In complete contrast to their London home, it is a typical farmhouse, which they have restored in perfect keeping with local traditions.

Opposite: The kitchen and breakfast room blend in with each other. The display of domestic utensils creates an almost theatrical feeling, while the overall mood is one of space and light tinged with a certain unmistakable Englishness.

Overleaf: Views such as this, often immortalized by the great painters of the past, have made Tuscany famous throughout the world.

a great deal into a small space without making it feel cluttered. There is a formal lawn whose space is broken intermittently by laurel bushes, then an area of natural sloping landscape covered in trees. The swimming pool appears to have been inspired by one in an ancient Roman villa, with a tiled surround, terra-cotta pots at its four corners, and a curving hedge at its head with a Classical bust in the center. There is also a paved area that is almost a summer house leading on to the lawn, and the occasional row of vines, a decorative feature on its roof, acts almost as an introduction to the vineyard that lies a short distance beyond. Everything is perfectly balanced along carefully gauged, organic lines.

The house is built of rough, unworked stone with no aesthetic pretensions. This stone, quarried in the surrounding hills, gives all the farmhouses in the area their solid, rugged appearance.

The old barn, its tiles pitted and darkened by time, leads into the house. The dining room has a fine nineteenth-century rectangular table and rustic chairs, a floor still composed of the old brick tiles, and the original beamed ceiling, giving the room an almost museum-like quality.

The real surprise, however, is the collection adorning the walls, the simple, almost abstract shapes of old farming implements that until only recently played their part in the daily work of the fields. It is a valuable collection, partly because of the single-minded way in which the owners combed the surrounding countryside in search of suitable pieces, but also because of the appreciation people have begun to show for these reminders of a bygone age, even to the point of creating museums of rustic life, particularly in small towns. The Wilsons' collection is one of the most interesting and comprehensive: winepresses, scythes, sickles, pitchforks, yokes and ploughs, all hung on the walls like splendidly eccentric decorative elements, demonstrating that even objects made for a purely functional purpose can possess an artistic dimension.

Above: Two glimpses of the garden, including the swimming pool in its unusual setting.

Right: Here, in the dining room, everything is a tribute or reference to the Chianti countryside. The owners are enthusiastic collectors of old farm implements, which they have used to turn this room into a sort of museum of local rustic life.

Opposite: A corner that captures the mood of the room, with a rustic clock that used to mark the passing of the hours, which, as everyone knows, go by at a very different rate in the country.

Opposite: This large rectangular room, originally a stable for livestock, has been transformed into a very elegant sitting room cleverly furnished so as to give a feeling of freedom and space. The rhythmical, ridged effect of the brick ceiling creates a strong sense of movement. The simple antique cupboard, almost two hundred years old, provides a tall, dark note in this otherwise pale, low-level room.

Right: Upstairs, another sitting room contains a carved dresser made specially for the owners. Its unusual shape is reminiscent of certain church furnishings of the seventeenth century. It takes the form of a niche containing some of the nineteenth-century china of which Judith Wilson is a passionate collector.

The old stables are now a light and airy sitting room covered by an unusual ceiling whose brickwork still retains its original concave rhythms. A simple fireplace graces the far wall of this room, which is divided into two areas and decorated in a light and delicate style that conveys a feeling of timeless elegance. Dominated by the imposing ceiling, the furnishings seem almost to fade into the background. Although the room is extensively furnished, the predominantly pale colour scheme makes it appear very spacious. The simple geometrics of the rugs, the pastels and whites of the armchairs, lamp and cushions, and the large mirror all contribute to the strong feeling of space and light. A nineteenth-century baby grand piano and a fine Tuscan cupboard, almost two hundred years old, provide the only decisive notes of solid solemnity.

Upstairs, another sitting room, formerly the farm kitchen, displays a much more eclectic style of decor, in which Tuscan items such as small pieces of nineteenth-century furniture, a large fireplace and a number of armchairs are mixed with Oriental elements like the two small chairs whose backs are made of buffalo horns. One corner of the room contains a niche specially made for the owners to display their fine collection of nineteenth-century china. The Wilsons'

Right: The decor of the owners' bedroom displays certain very English elements, such as the white bed with its fabric hangings.

Opposite: Another view of the bedroom, the floor of which is almost completely covered by a white rug. The small wardrobe adds a further touch of elegance, while the wooden stairs leading up to a low gallery enhance the feeling of space. The rustic ceiling beams are a reminder of the house's Tuscan origins. Strong, bright light floods the room through a small window that overlooks the rolling countryside. The whole house radiates that same quality of quiet simplicity described in the countless short stories that enrich the literary heritage of Tuscany.

Below: A small but very elegant bookcase, which contains the Wilsons' most precious books, lines the corridor between two rooms in the house.

bedroom is a sea of white: the delicately embroidered bedding, the rug, the small table, the sofa and the walls. Their daughter's simply furnished bedroom is a pale pink; a pillow embroidered with her name, Daisy, adds a charming touch.

Il Prato is a treasure house of memories and echoes of far-off England, but it is also a respectful, heartfelt tribute to the enduring traditions of Tuscany. The owners' love of Tuscany shines through every corner of the house: in the dining room, a veritable museum of traditional peasant life; in the kitchen, which reflects and glorifies local traditions; and in the ceilings with their massive beams, the same ones that gave shelter to countless generations of Tuscan farmers.

126

FATTORIA DI CASTAGNOLI

Castagnoli is a fortified hilltown consisting of a few houses grouped around a solid rock, encircled by a set of walls and dominated by an elegantly linear villa set amid rolling lawns. Around it stretches a geometrical landscape of vineyards, lines of green on a fertile, stony ground, followed by a clump of trees punctuated by cypresses and, a few steps away, a small church. The whole thing is linked by a narrow road winding through this group of hills in the Chianti countryside.

Castagnoli is first mentioned in documents dating from as early as 930. As a Florentine stronghold it also took part in the struggles between Siena and Florence, and in 1478 its small but valiant population was involved in violent skirmishes with Sienese troops and with the Aragonese soldiers of the king of Naples. It was a time of heroism and bloody sacrifice, but things altered radically in 1555, when the proud Sienese republic fell to the Florentines and became part of the Grand Duchy of Tuscany. That event marked the end of a brutal and deadly chapter in the history of the small fortified town. Austere defensive structures now began to assume the characteristics of a residential complex; large numbers of windows

Above: Castagnoli, which appears on the horizon like a sudden outcrop of stone amidst the rolling green hills of Sienese Chianti, was once made up of a castle and a fortified town. Like many other hill towns of its type, it took part in the wars between Florence and Siena, whose battles were frequently fought in the Chianti countryside. Today Castagnoli retains its fortifications, together with its great rock and old houses. During the eighteenth century, an elegantly proportioned villa was built by the Tempi family just a short distance from the town.

Opposite: The eighteenth-century villa is surrounded by a garden bereft of any statuary or other man-made elements.

were cut into the rough stone walls to brighten the interiors.

The new proprietors had always possessed vast landholdings in the area. Families as illustrious as the Piccolomini, the Tempi, and the Ricasoli followed each other as owners of the small town and of the beautiful house, which was not built until the eighteenth century, when the surrounding countryside became a major grape- and wine-producing area. The town had already been producing excellent wine since the Middle Ages, but the main emphasis was now on full-scale production by the cellar, which in the meantime had become one of the most famous in the area. Even Grand Duke Pietro Leopoldo of Lorraine, on the occasion of his visit to Chianti in July 1773, wrote: "The Castagnoli property belonging to the Tempi is excellently maintained . . . and the peasants live well."

The rock, the town and the elegant villa, with its original and well-proportioned design, have for some time now been the property of the Milanese lawyer Calogero Cali, who has made extensive improvements to its vineyard and winery. A keen patron of the arts, Cali is particularly fond of paintings, so his home is

filled with canvases by both old masters and contemporary artists. Every wall in the house displays something of interest.

The house stands almost at the center of a vast garden. Tall cypresses and fir trees break up the large surrounding lawn that extends to the modern swimming pool of unusual design. The interior contains forty rooms, some of which have been partly altered and opened into each other; although the rooms are now fewer they are larger. The front door leads into a series of interconnecting rooms, and almost every corner of the house contains that characteristic feature of noble buildings: a fireplace. The one standing at the end of the corridor is made entirely of brick with a mantelpiece in the form of an old beam on which rest two Empire vases and a fine nineteenth-century clock. A small adjoining room with a brick ceiling has an equally simple fireplace decorated with many bottles neatly arranged as though for an exhibition. One wall displays the fantastic, unrestrained colours of a still life by Cascella, as well as a canvas by Aligi Sassu, with his typically distorted, elongated figures bursting with life. On another wall, a seventeenth-century painting of the Roman school depicting a soft-eyed young flautist contrasts with the work of a contemporary artist, A. Alfieri.

On the upper floor there is an almost endless succession of bedrooms and other rooms. A beautiful *salotto* with a large

Above and below: Another view of the house and the fine eighteenth-century doorway, framed by blocks of rusticated stone, that leads into the rooms on the ground floor.

Left: Beyond the swimming pool the house's vast grounds stretch into a breathtaking view that takes in the surrounding countryside.

fireplace and an eighteenth-century beamed ceiling provides an ideal place to entertain guests. The warmth of the room is enhanced by the gentle beams of the ceiling, the original floor of large brick blocks, the comfortable sofas and armchairs and the display of small silver objects in the nineteenth-century cabinet set into the wall. The room also contains two fine paintings depicting musical instruments, including a guitar, a violin, a viola and a harpsichord, portrayed with that descriptive freshness characteristic of this sort of seventeenth-century Italian work.

In the adjacent dining room the owner's collection of seventeenth-century still lifes continues. One of them, which occupies almost the whole of one wall, is a true visual feast painted with a perfectionist's attention to detail: luscious bunches of grapes, mouth-watering pears, delectable melons and pomegranates, are arrayed before a background of classical ruins. On another wall hangs a less gentle genre painting depicting a plucked chicken, sides of meat, sausages and a few vegetables. Both paintings have beautiful contemporary frames.

The long corridor that wends its labyrinthine way through every part of the building is more than just a means of linking different rooms: it is a veritable gallery of drawings and watercolours by Renato Guttuso, whose favourite subject

Above: This attractive corner in one of the large reception rooms houses a nineteenth-century display cabinet set into the wall and containing precious silver objects. On either side, a painting of the seventeenth-century Italian school depicts musical instruments.

Opposite: Labyrinthine corridors link an endless succession of rooms, most of which possess a fireplace. This rustic brick example, whose beamed mantelpiece supports two small Empire-style vases, alludes to the fact that the ground floor once housed the stables as well as the presses used for making wine and olive oil.

is the female form. Another *salotto*, again with a fireplace, offers a symmetrically arranged display of sixteenth-century still lifes with two works depicting floral subjects. Painted in an elegant, almost "sketchy" style of painting, they are the work of the French painter Blain de Fontenay. Like the other staircases in the house, this one, with its steel framework and pale stone steps, is a modern insertion that blends perfectly with the timelessness of the massive walls, the furniture, and the rest of the decor.

The Castagnoli estate, one of the most

revival in fortunes achieved through a radical transformation of existing working practises. The introduction of the latest wine-making techniques, the enlargement of its infrastructure, and a highly selective choice of vineyard have all enabled the estate to become one of the most prestigious in the area. In addition to its winery, Castagnoli's almost 30 hectares (75 acres) of olive grove also allow for the production of considerable amounts of high-quality olive oil.

This villa with its rapid succession of welcoming rooms and its feeling of elegant restraint, is another gem of the Chianti region, rescued and brought back to life by a Milanese lawyer of Sicilian descent who loves Tuscany more than anywhere else in the world.

important grape- and wine-producing enterprises in Chianti, covers an area of 980 hectares (2,420 acres), of which 58 (143 acres) are devoted to the production of Chianti Classico. That the production has reached this sort of level is a tribute to the enthusiasm of Cali, who bought the estate when it was in severe difficulties and, within the space of a few years, succeeded in relaunching its wines on both the Italian and international markets, a

Above: This perspective view shows the simple beauty of the vaulted brick ceiling, which has been left in its original state.

Right: In the dining room, the eye is drawn to this eighteenth-century commode, above which hangs a still life that perfectly reflects the mood of the room.

Opposite: A modern staircase, which harmonizes perfectly with the rest of the house, leads to the upper floor, where the seemingly endless warren of rooms continues.

FATTORIA IL GREPPO

Every detail in the great kitchen of the Fattoria Il Greppo reflects the feeling of Tuscany and is a tribute to its craftsmen. The original cooking range, however, is the most evocative feature, a shrine to gastronomy, an architectural element dedicated to hospitality. Its four columns, its small series of stone steps and its fittings in chestnut and cypress wood create a small monument, a symbolic meeting place around which people can communicate, exchange views and enjoy each other's company. The arch-shaped glazed door, the simple nineteenth-century rectangular table and the old marble washbasin surrounded by hundred-year-old copper pots whose burnished surfaces glitter with reflected light, also play their part in giving the room its special atmosphere.

The villa and its cellar are renowned throughout the world. The vineyards stretching across the surrounding countryside, some terraced in the traditional Tuscan way, produce Brunello di Montalcino, one of the world's best-loved wines. This wine was, in fact, created at the end of the last century by Ferruccio Biondi Santi, the grandfather of the current owner, Franco Biondi Santi.

Above: This romantic glimpse of the garden from one of the windows of Il Greppo shows the goldfish pond. Beyond it the cypresses, an inalienable part of the Tuscan landscape, cast their lengthy shadows.

Opposite: From a distance, the house seems to shrink into a circle of trees. Around it stretches a vast architecture of vineyards, where after several attempts a wine was produced at the beginning of the century that was subsequently to become one of the world's favourites. That wine, Brunello di Montalcino, is still a source of great pride for the Biondi Santi family.

The hospitable owners and the memories of the family's illustrious forebears give the house its unique quality, a mixture of English style and Tuscan tradition. The small, elegant house is a sort of cross between a noble villa and a prosperous country home. Its seventeenth-century origins are verified by contemporary documents and by several architectural details: brickwork arches, buttressed walls and elegant ceiling decorations. At the beginning of this century, however, the building was extensively enlarged and refurbished.

The new architectural additions are particularly noticeable from the garden, which revolves around an elegant pool surrounded by six columns topped with flower-filled urns. Plump goldfish swim lazily among the waterlilies in undisturbed peace. The garden used to contain the fine geometrical beds characteristic of the Italian style, but for reasons of maintenance it was transformed into a simpler but equally attractive English garden. The green expanse of the lawn is enclosed by a low stone wall, while the facade overlooking the garden is stained dark green by the ivy that clambers all over the house. The compact, organic quality of

Opposite: The great kitchen is also a typically Tuscan dining room, with an elegant glazed door set in an arch, a large cooking range, a nineteenth-century table, a marble sink and a selection of copper pots and pans.

Right: The old marble sink now makes a fine decorative feature.

Below: A detail of the cooking range. This dramatic feature is not only used for cooking; it is, above all, a place around which guests gather to enjoy each other's company.

the main body of the building is enlivened by a terrace leading off a small archway.

One particularly evocative room is the owner's study, in which a fireplace with a highly original circular cowl seems to fulfil a similar role to the one in the kitchen; in fact, the nineteenth-century bench running around the edge makes an ideal place for conversation. Opposite, a nineteenth-century sink runs along the wall, and to one side are a number of family photographs of Signor Biondi Santi with his wife Maria Floria, his children, his father and his friends. Books are scattered everywhere and lithographs of the house line the wall. The room is warm, welcoming, and very lively; despite its small size, it conveys a great feeling of space.

There is one room for which the owners feel a particular affection. It used to belong to Tancredi Biondi Santi, the present owner's father, who was one of Italy's greatest wine growers and whose memory still lives on in this room. Everything has been left as it was: a nineteenth-century velvet sofa, a small nineteenth-century writing desk and a decorative frieze of intertwined vines running around the top of the wall.

A wooden staircase leads to the upper floor, where a large *salotto* greets guests with a feeling of unpretentious elegance. A small glazed cabinet contains a display of hunting guns and a few military guns

Left: The entire surface of the facade overlooking the garden is covered in green. The villa's exterior clearly reveals the way it has grown over the years, right up to certain obviously nineteenth-century additions.

Below: A small *salotto* on the upper floor, perhaps the most interesting room in the house, contains these three brickwork arches, rescued with considerable foresight from the structure of the original building. The arches echo the essential qualities of Sienese architecture.

from the last century, which belonged to Ferruccio Biondi Santi, the owner's grandfather, who in his youth fought alongside Garibaldi.

Another small *salotto*, almost an antechamber, is enlivened by a small early-nineteenth-century piano, which functions as a beautiful piece of furniture rather than a musical instrument. Three small steps lead up to the most interesting room in the house: another *salotto*, containing a fine Empire sofa and a small masterpiece by Ferruccio Biondi Santi, a "landscape of stone," a subject that recurred in many of his works. Ferrucio, despite all his other activities, also found time to devote himself to painting with considerable success. A particularly interesting feature of this room are the three brick arches, remains of the earlier structure, which create an almost theatrical sense of perspective.

The Biondi Santi estate is also a great

Left: The study reflects the busy life of Franco Biondi Santi: books, documents, mementoes on the walls and a fireplace with a hood that repeats the spirit, if not the design, of the range in the kitchen.

Below: This corridor, which links various rooms on the upper floor, has been treated like the *salotto* of some noble house.

history. As time went by, many other winemakers in the area began producing high-quality Brunello, but, even after a hundred years, the Brunello par excellence is still that produced by the Biondi Santi, the family whose ancestor's scholarly spirit and lengthy research first

wine-producing enterprise, one of the many cellars producing Brunello di Montalcino, of which there are now almost two hundred in this small patch of land. This is one of the many famous Tuscan labels exported throughout the world as ambassadors of the region's finest wines. During the second part of the nineteenth century Ferruccio Biondi Santi replanted the new vineyards with a single variety of vine and, using these grapes exclusively, created a full-bodied wine with a gentle bouquet, a rounded taste and a reddish-brown colour. It was called "Brunello" and then "di Montalcino," after the nearby medieval town. Over the years its success grew, but the owners made a conscious decision not to increase production, preferring instead to cherish a wine that would always be the same as the one created by Ferruccio. This has enabled them to avoid the tyranny of market forces and become a part of

created it, achieving results that continue to satisfy even the most demanding palate.

Left: This staircase – similar in construction to the ones found in old farmhouses, which often led up to the pigeon loft – symbolizes the owners' desire to express their affection for all things Tuscan, even the smallest details.

Opposite: The stylish library is the elegant creation of Tuscan master craftsmen. The restful shades of the garden, only a step away, create a gentle contrast with the strong browns of the library.

Right: An elegant room with ceiling decorations and furnishings in the nineteenth-century taste, this room is Franco Biondi Santi's tribute to his father, Tancredi, one of the most famous wine makers of the early twentieth century. The study used to be his, and everything has been left as it was during his lifetime.

CASA LO SBARCATELLO

A strong love of the sea had led London yachtsman John Vestey to travel the waters of every part of the world. As soon as he could snatch a free moment from his work he would weigh anchor and point the slender keel of his sailboat in the direction of some far-off destination. It was a passion that had no end, an emotion that never failed to stir him.

One day in May 1977, he was sailing along the Tuscan coastline of the Tyrrhenian Sea. The gulf of Porto Ercole, with its small town set amid the gently rolling terrain, was already in sight, but he decided to make a brief stop in a tiny, inviting bay. The boat came to a standstill just a few meters from land. The anchor had already reached the bottom.

As he looked up, his eyes were greeted by a lush, evocative landscape to which he felt strangely drawn. He disembarked and, a few steps away, encountered an old farmhouse whose buildings exuded an aura of nobility (indeed, it once belonged to the princely Borghese family). Had he perhaps found the place for which he had been searching for so many years? The place in which he could finally settle down?

Surrounded by luxuriant olive trees,

Above: The main entrance, framed by a monumental travertine surround, makes a splendid introduction to this elegant house with its maritime feel, whose details reflect its owners' love of the sea.

Opposite: The Casa Lo Sbarcatello looks out over the bay of the same name. It was here after a long voyage, that John Vestey's yacht touched land, forever to remain. Its natural setting of eucalyptuses, olive trees and prickly pears, with an occasional cypress almost touching the sea, possesses the same feeling of unfettered freedom that has always inspired this expert sailor, who has finally come to rest in these surroundings for which he had always been subconsciously searching. The sea still forms part of his life, now as something to be admired from the terrace of the house.

sturdy, wind-blown holm oaks and exotic eucalyptuses, John Vestey, the perennial sailor who had always lived close to the sea, in Australia, South Africa, Spain and many other countries, decided to settle here, a short distance from Porto Ercole, in the bay of Lo Sbarcatello, on the very edge of Tuscany, in this house that he was seeing for the first time but which he felt was already his. He acquired it two years later, and since then he has lived here with his companion, Judith, Countess Bathurst, who is also English and who shares his passion for the sea.

A small courtyard surrounding a beautiful well – now a small pond filled with waterlilies – opens up the main facade and gives it a feeling of space. The long, low facade, which fronts a ground floor and an upper floor, reflects the stylistic variety of the building, a cross between a Tuscan farmhouse and a country villa. The sea is close at hand, however, and, particularly in the broad, overhanging design of the monumental windows one senses a remote echo of Spanish and Moorish influences. The same influence can be detected, often in a much more pronounced way, in several

CASA LO SBARCATELLO

Far left: At the center of the courtyard in front of the main facade stands an old well, its stonework enlivened by a rich growth of greenery. It is now a sort of miniature pond, with beautiful waterlilies growing in its waters.

Left: The facade overlooking the sea resembles that of a Tuscan farmhouse, even though the building has in fact always been a small country villa and for a long time belonged to the princely Borghese family from Rome.

Above: This charming eighteenth-century bas-relief, which hangs on one of the outside walls, is a fine example of a traditional Tuscan form of exterior design.

Opposite below: The lush vegetation that reaches down to the waters of the bay of Lo Sbarcatello in the gulf of Porto Ercole is here interrupted by the buildings and courtyard of John Vestey's house. Midway between a Tuscan farmhouse and a villa, its architectural elegance is emphasized by such monumental features as the well head and the doorway.

Right: The entrance hall, with its table display of small family objects, is a haven of memories. On the wall hang several delicate watercolours painted by Judith, Countess Bathurst, a talented artist. The owner's dog poses contentedly on the rug. The hall leads into the other rooms on the ground floor, the most outstanding of which is the great *salotto*.

other old houses of the region.

Around the courtyard grows a mixture of olive trees, eucalyptuses and prickly pears, a combination that mirrors the natural flora of this coastline. A monumental travertine surround frames the splendid doorway, creating a feeling of grandeur and anticipation, while on one of the walls an attractive eighteenth-century bas-relief, perhaps of the Tuscan or Roman school, displays the charming figures of two putti holding a swag of flowers and reclining on a grotesque mask. The ground floor contains a number of rooms, many of which flow directly into each other through open arches.

The entrance hall possesses several fine decorative features, including a small nineteenth-century Tuscan table, a gilt mirror and several period prints. A welcoming *salotto*, which leads off to the right, contains a set of simple

Opposite: In the *salotto*, a large antique tapestry covers part of the wall, while the old but still solid beams create a dramatically graphic effect on the ceiling. The room radiates a simple, unforced elegance.

Right and below right: The bedroom is undoubtedly the room that most clearly proclaims the owners' English origins; the rustic beams of the ceiling are perhaps the only truly Tuscan element. The white bed with its row of pillows, the small table with its collection of memorabilia, and the overall sense of light are all typically English features. The wooden headboard, the eighteenth-century chest of drawers, and the highly decorative writing desk – another eighteenth-century piece – all enhance the romantic mood of the room.

Below: Three etchings by Salvador Dalí hang beside the fireplace in the upstairs *salotto*, a tribute to the extraordinary genius of the great Spanish artist.

bookshelves, an antique tapestry and two attractive nineteenth-century armchairs.

Upstairs, the bedroom proclaims its owners' English origins: pervaded by a typically English sense of neatness and order, the room features a rococo-style writing desk and a decorative table bearing a mass of small objects acquired over the years in various parts of the world. The dark wood of the ceiling beams, the headboard, and the eighteenth-century

Left: The simply furnished dining room recalls the style of the 1930s.

Opposite: Upstairs there is another large *salotto*, dominated by this massive stone fireplace, which has recently been restored. The wall beside the fireplace is decorated with the Dalí etchings. A particularly fine cabinet, a collector's piece of the seventeenth-century Spanish school, is in keeping with the elements of Hispano-Moresque influence in the house (the region was conquered by the Spaniards and the Moors on several occasions). This room leads on to a beautiful terrace overlooking the lush coastal vegetation and the sea, which John Vestey still contemplates with love, but with no feelings of regret.

chest of drawers strike a note of contrast with the predominantly pale colour scheme.

The elegantly proportioned *salotto*, which projects a completely different and much more animated atmosphere, boasts a splendid Spanish cabinet decorated with hand-worked bas-reliefs. A signed etching by Salvador Dalí catches the eye, as does the stone fireplace, which, despite clear signs of restoration, still retains its beauti-

ful rustic design. The most modern feature in the house is the dining room, with its attractive 1930s-style chairs and table.

Beyond the building is an elegant lawn whose green expanse is dotted with stone slabs to create a sort of open-air *salotto*. Because the owners generally stay at Lo Sbarcatello during the hottest months (spending the rest of the year in London), they often eat outside in the cool sea air,

seated at a long table beneath a pergola.

As dusk falls and the sun disappears into the sea, the contours of the house gradually fade into the background and Lo Sbarcatello slumbers in the company of its owner, for whom it is a lasting love affair built of stone, an attachment strong enough to make John Vestey leave behind the solid mast of his sailboat, a boat that has come to rest forever in this small, beautiful bay in the Tyrrhenian Sea.

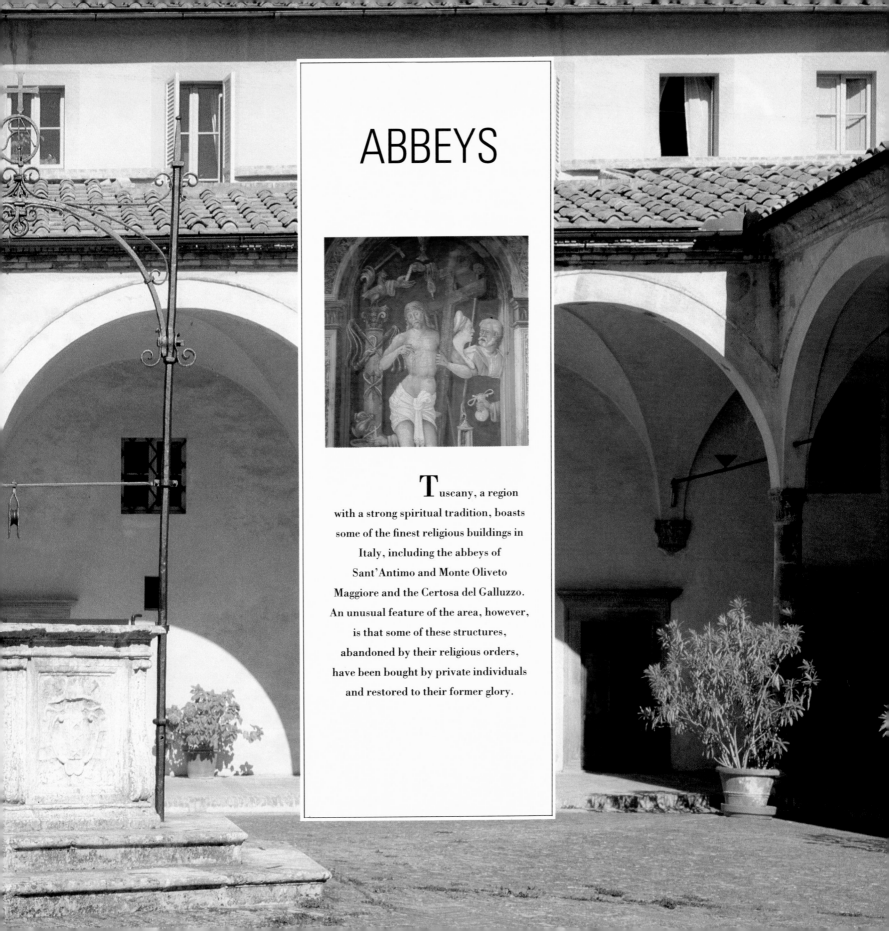

ABBEYS

Tuscany, a region
with a strong spiritual tradition, boasts
some of the finest religious buildings in
Italy, including the abbeys of
Sant'Antimo and Monte Oliveto
Maggiore and the Certosa del Galluzzo.
An unusual feature of the area, however,
is that some of these structures,
abandoned by their religious orders,
have been bought by private individuals
and restored to their former glory.

BADIA A COLTIBUONO

Although the monks, with their ascetic faces perpetually veiled in prayer, have abandoned the solid walls of Badia a Coltibuono, they have left behind them a mute stone representative, discovered by chance during earlier restoration work. This small figure of an old monk, with beautiful, time-worn features, now stands by the entrance to the closed portico that runs round the fifteenth-century cloister.

The owners of the Badia are highly cultured and the building often plays host to musical performances and parties. Above all, however, it is a historic winery that has lost none of its original vocation of silence. There is a feeling of stillness and timelessness, a mood of decorative restraint that leaves no room for frivolity. Though now a private home, this is still an abbey that retains its original character.

In 770 a Florentine noble, Geremia dei Firidolfi, fell under the spell of this cool, wooded spot and ordered a church with adjoining oratory to be built there. The complex radiates a feeling of spirituality and seems to have been designed specifically for peaceful meditation. The first recluses arrived, seeking refuge from the

Above: The church and campanile are the oldest elements of Badia a Coltibuono. A large door to the right opens into a courtyard enclosed within eighteenth-century walls. The surrounding countryside extends into a wood that was first planted by the Benedictine monks.

Opposite: The garden facade of the Stucchi Prinetti family's house is covered in greenery. It overlooks the elegant shapes of the Italian garden, which is like an open-air room furnished with the rhythmical, linear movement of box hedges and bushes, a tribute to the fertile imagination of its designer. The owners are proud of this green corner, which represents the gentler side of a building that otherwise makes no concessions to light-heartedness and frivolity.

temptations of a corrupt, insidious world. Then the original buildings fell into disrepair until, in 1058, the pope himself, Nicholas II, arrived at the monastery to consecrate a new Romanesque church.

In the meantime, Benedictine monks of the Vallombrosa order had settled there and, mindful of one of the many maxims of their founding father, set about cultivating the land. They planted vines and olives and established a dense wood of oaks, chestnuts and pines. Today, apart from the campanile and the church, the buildings are partly fifteenth-century and partly from later centuries, with the central section dating from the fifteenth century. A certain Abbot Paolo da Montemignaio began building the cloister in 1427, and the corridor on the first floor, along which the small cells of the monks are strung out like rosary beads, also dates from the same period. The two wings, however, and the walled surround with its broad entrance arch granting access to the courtyard, date from 1710. The enclosure of the fifteenth-century cloister took place at a much later date.

That slow life, whose tempo was regulated by precise rules accepted in a spirit of quiet obedience, a life of work, deep-

Far left: Another view of the building, this time from the garden.

Left: The entrance block to the body of the monastery proper, whose facade is built entirely of rough stone, contains a doorway with a rusticated surround.

Below: This overview shows the rhythmical design of the garden, with its artificial terraces, its relaxation areas and its cadences of natural elements. Despite its feeling of spontaneity, this layout is the result of precise and careful thought.

rooted faith and spiritual contemplation, was interrupted after seven centuries by a peremptory edict issued by Napoleon. In 1810, as further confirmation of his scant sympathy for the clerical world, he suppressed the monastery of Badia a Coltibuono, together with many of Italy's other historical religious foundations. It was a bitter blow, bringing with it the danger of the Badia being abandoned and consigned to oblivion. A centuries-old tradition was at risk of being broken by the impetuous edict of an emperor more interested in conquest than spiritual enlightenment. But the Badia's destiny was governed by favourable stars. The property passed through the hands of the Girauds, then the Poniatowskis and the Giuntini, and finally the Stucchi Prinetti. They were sympathetic, sensitive owners who retained the Badia's original religious character. They made no disfiguring alterations, they did not transform

Right: On one of the courtyard walls of the grotto, a lion's mask spouts water into a small basin.

Below: The fifteenth-century character of the property's nucleus is proclaimed by this small, secluded courtyard, whose square shape has a spare, graphic quality in its almost total lack of embellishment. The well at the center, which now acts purely as a visual feature, was once one of the mainstays of the monastery's life when it was used to collect rainwater for the monks.

rooms that had been made for prayer, nor did they add unnecessary frills to the flat, monochrome walls found in so many of its rooms. Even more exceptionally, they retained the intellectual design of the Italian garden, making no attempt to follow the fashion for English-style lawns, which, however beautiful, are at complete variance with the traditional spirit of the Italian garden.

The old church is still a very popular setting for weddings, and the parish priest frequently celebrates Mass there. The convex shape of its small apse greets visitors arriving by the narrow, winding road that leads up to the broad plateau containing the Badia and the starkly linear shape of its medieval tower. The main entrance leads into a scene of rustic elegance: the eighteenth-century courtyard, the noble sixteenth-century facade of the abbot's palace, and, in the background, the buildings of the farmhouse.

The interior of the palace has a soothing, restful quality. In the dim light one's eye takes in the peaceful decor of a small dining room and the comforting spaciousness of the kitchen. The *salotto* has been restored and refurbished by the architect Franco Albini, who also worked on other areas of the palace. It is an unostentatious room designed to be lived in. The focal point is the fireplace, around which are ranged a sofa and armchairs. There is also a picturesque, typically Tuscan

Above: In the *salone degli stucchi*, a wooden angel of considerable size supports an even larger candelabra. This eighteenth-century wooden sculpture is a delightfully original work that, thanks to its dimensions and its grace, has become the dominant feature of the room.

Right: Monks once ate their silent, frugal meals in this refectory, which still retains its tranquil, rarefied atmosphere. It has a rib-vaulted ceiling, wall frescoes depicting the twelve abbots who administered the abbey, and, on the far wall, three frescoes narrating episodes from the life of San Lorenzo, the patron saint of Coltibuono. There is also a relaxation area, complete with sofa and armchairs. During the summer months, the silence of the great refectory is broken by the melodious sounds of the famous musicians taking part in the busy concert season.

corner, where an old marble mortar, its grainy surface now grey with age, rests on a series of three stone steps leading up to a window, placed high in the wall overlooking the courtyard.

A large eighteenth-century wooden figure of an angel, whose face has the barely formed features and chubby cheeks of a child, struggles to support a candelabra. This attractive and highly decorative sculpture, with its rather unusual iconography, stands in the *salotto degli stucchi*, so called because of its delicate rococo wall decorations created by German monks who stayed at the abbey during the eighteenth century as a way of thanking the abbot for his hospitality.

The walls of the old refectory display a rhythmical series of fresco lunettes contained within the niches formed by the upward sweep of the ribbed vaulting; these depict the solemn faces of the twelve abbots who headed the abbey through the years. The far wall portrays three episodes from the life of San Lorenzo, the patron saint of Coltibuono; this work has been tentatively attributed to the Mannerist painter and fresco artist Bernardino Poccetti, who also worked at the court of the Medici.

The refectory is a perfect room: warm, restrained, and furnished in a way that is both in keeping with its earlier function and provides an appropriate setting for its splendid series of frescoes. During the summer it is used for concerts attended by the owners' friends and by people living in the neighbourhood. The musicians, who often include world-renowned figures, play for sheer enjoyment and there is none of that feeling of exclusivity found in concert halls. Thanks to the room's wonderful acoustics, the notes achieve perfect pitch and harmony.

The fifteenth-century courtyard, frozen in time, still retains its ancient layout and its age-old mood of gentle spirituality. The monks' cells on the ground floor, which have lost their original austerity and been adapted to accommodate the needs of lesser mortals, now act as small bedrooms for the many friends who visit the owners and their family. On the wall of the corridor a magnificent, recently restored fresco depicts the *Lamentation of the Crucified Christ by the Two Marys, San Lorenzo and San Giovanni*

Above: The two long corridors of the portico form a perfect square enclosing the little cloister.

Left: Christ with the Virgin Mary, Mary Magdalene and Saints Lorenzo and Giovanni Gualberto appear in this important fresco, recently restored by the present owners to its former glory. It has been attributed to the sixteenth-century master Francesco D'Ubertino, better known as Il Bachiacca. The most interesting work of art in the Badia a Coltibuono, it reflects the Flemish influences that characterize Il Bachiacca's early works.

Gualberto. The excellent narrative quality of this sixteenth-century work, has led to suggestions that it may be by Francesco d'Ubertino, called Il Bachiacca, a Florentine artist strongly influenced by contemporary Flemish painters. The same name has also been put forward for the fresco of *Christ at the Pillar* in the library, formerly the monks' chapel.

A visit to the Italian garden completes our tour of the Badia. Its box hedges, clipped into broad cones and balls or geometric lines in a subtle interplay of rationality and fantasy, are a triumphant example of the Italian style of formal garden.

Badia a Coltibuono is a place to be savoured at leisure; any idea of speed does not belong here. Its initial impact evokes a response of awe and respect, then, as the walls become familiar, the visitor gradually discovers something that excites much more than mere admiration. The rarefied atmosphere of the Benedictines lingers on, and even just a brief stay in its surroundings will lift one's spirits.

This is also a place of work, however, in which a happy marriage has been achieved between traditional and modern methods of farming. Old processes that guarantee good quality are not forgotten,

Right: The beamed ceiling, the large marble-topped island, and the assortment of copper cooking utensils hanging from a wooden frame all enhance the traditional atmosphere of this spacious kitchen, one of the favourite rooms of the mistress of the house, Lorenza Stucchi de'Medici. A noted food expert and writer on gastronomic affairs, she often runs courses on Italian cookery – with particular emphasis on Tuscan cuisine – for groups of foreigners who stay at the Badia in the old monks' cells. These have now been turned into bedrooms that are comfortable without being luxurious, in accordance with the overall decorative mood of the building that still retains the subtly monastic spirit of an abbey.

Opposite: The old chapel of the monks is now a library filled with books. Its far wall is dominated by the sole surviving element of a now-vanished altar, a fresco depicting *Christ at the Pillar*. Displaying strong Flemish influences, it is rich in symbolic allusions, but its attribution is still the subject of discussion. Some scholars believe it be to by the early-sixteenth century Florentine master Francesco d'Ubertino, called Il Bachiacca, who was responsible for another fresco on the wall of the first-floor corridor. Others believe it is the work of a Flemish artist, probably a monk staying in the Badia at the time.

Right: The cloistered atmosphere pervades every corner of the Badia, but it is particularly noticeable in this long corridor on the first floor. On the left are the doors leading into the monks' cells, which have now been transformed into small guest bedrooms.

Below: In the dining room, this simple cabinet of the seventeenth-century Tuscan school stands out for the rarity of its design.

but new techniques are also exploited. Coltibuono, was already producing very high-quality wines when the market suffered a period of uncertainty during the 1960s, so a decision was made to embark on a process of innovation to further improve their wines. Today, the example set by Badia a Coltibuono has been followed by almost all the best-known wine-producing concerns.

Wines, oil and grappa are all guaranteed by an experience that spans many generations. But their quality is also partly due to the very favourable location of the fields, situated on a strip of land that receives a great deal of sun. It is as though the credit for their success is due not only to the present-day owners, but also to Geremia dei Firidolfi, the man responsible for building the earliest nucleus of what would later become one of the most romantic properties on Tuscan soil.

CERTOSA DI MAGGIANO

When Signora Anna Grossi Recordati first saw the Certosa di Maggiano, she vowed that one day it would be hers. At that time she was living in Siena, where her husband, heart surgeon Professor Adalberto Grossi, had become rector of the university. Although a native of Milan like her husband, she still found life in the small Tuscan town too hectic. She needed completely different surroundings, somewhere she could find peace and quiet, a place where, for the first time, she would be able to enjoy a life steeped in silence. Her husband had his misgivings, but he was gradually won over by his wife's insistence, and in 1969 the Certosa di Maggiano, an entire monastic complex standing at the gates of Siena, was finally theirs.

It was an adventurous decision, some would say a gamble. The ancient monastery was in a terrible state: the original design of its great cloister was almost completely hidden by unsightly additions, its fourteenth-century ceilings concealed by later walls. Over the centuries the entire complex had been disfigured by insensitive alterations that had destroyed part of its appealing, sober layout. During the Second World War several families had

Above: Although the monastery belongs to the Grossi Recordati family, the church remains under ecclesiastical control and Mass is still celebrated there. This monumental door is opened only on special days to welcome the faithful; the rest of the time it remains shut.

Opposite: Carthusian monasteries, which enjoyed particular success in Tuscany, were always planned with two cloisters. The smaller one, illustrated here, has been skilfully restored by the owners. The other cloister was destroyed during the mid nineteenth century. The bell tower is clearly an eighteenth-century addition, but everything else has remained as it once was and still retains its former mystical appearance. The paving of the courtyard, with its herringbone pattern of small bricks, is the same one that was trodden by the monks in days gone by.

taken up residence in it, living in conditions of considerable discomfort, with only the barest essentials needed for survival. Signora Grossi Recordati, however, sensed that all this could be changed to reveal the pure, clean architectural lines of a group of buildings designed for a life of prayer and meditation.

There was more than enough space for herself, her husband and her five children; in fact, there was too much. And so one wing of the complex became the family home, while the other wing was converted into a hotel. This hotel, a member of the Relais et Châteaux chain, is furnished with meticulous attention to Tuscan decor.

St Bruno, the founder of the Carthusian order, had already been dead for two hundred years, but his enlightened teachings still lived on in the hearts and minds of many pious men. Charterhouses (*certose*, Carthusian monasteries) sprang up throughout Europe, all displaying a similar architectural style inspired by a precise layout that called for two adjacent cloisters, a church with a nearby cluster of small cells for the monks. Riccardo Petroni, a jurisconsult from Siena who

Left: The portico, which once enclosed the great cloister, displays a rhythmical series of slender pillars. Here, during the hot summer months, lunch is served to guests at the Certosa.

Center: The surviving cloister now acts as a sort of open-air living room, where people can sit back and relax.

Below: At the center of the cloister stands an old well that, in less polluted days, collected the pure rainwater that was used by the monks for their countless daily chores. The arches of the portico that dominate the well head create a feeling of perfect symmetry, while the small windows overlooking the courtyard belong to the rooms that the monks, in an act of spiritual submission, called their "cells."

Right: This view shows the considerable size of the Certosa: the compact body of the church, the elegant bell tower, the portico and the site of the great cloister, now replaced by a large lawn. The column at the center, once the hub of the cloister, now gives a monumental note to the simple lawn, where guests relax on deckchairs in the warm spring sun and admire the countryside: a landscape on small hills that leads into a dense wood and then roams free through meadows, fields and streams.

Overleaf: Little groups of buildings are scattered throughout the Tuscan countryside, with a few houses clustered together or, as in this view, linked together by fields and low hills.

became a cardinal under Pope Boniface VIII, bequeathed a large sum of money for the building of four monasteries, and the first to be built in Tuscany was the Certosa di Maggiano, work on which began in 1316 (followed shortly afterwards by the nearby Certosa di Pontignano). Time passed serenely for the monks, the rhythm of its life governed by the precise rules of an imposed routine: prayer, scripture reading, work in the fields.

A life of this sort was one of the paths to sainthood, and one of the cardinal's relatives, seventeen-year-old Pietro Petroni, entered the monastery and became a living saint after only a few years. People flocked to this man, who had a word of enlightenment for everyone, and the number of miracles due to his intercession grew apace. During the sixteenth century the complex became involved in the bitter war between Emperor Charles V of Spain and Henri II of France that affected the whole of Europe. The monastery emerged from the conflict with broken bones, but, although partly destroyed, it did not die. It was quickly rebuilt and reconsecrated in 1623, while in the mid eighteenth century a new bell tower was erected to replace the earlier one that had fallen into disrepair.

The monks continued their tranquil existence until 1782, when Grand Duke Leopold of Tuscany thought of turning

Left: The reading room, furnished entirely with highly imaginative pieces created by the architect Enzo Mongiardino, has a large bookcase of alder, walnut sofas upholstered in silk and an unusual lamp based on a nineteenth-century design.

Opposite: The walls of the elegant *Sala degli Imperatori*, which was also furnished throughout by Mongiardino, display a series of twelve eighteenth-century Venetian portraits of ancient Roman emperors. This room more than any other recalls the former role of the Certosa. The ceiling still retains its original vaulting beneath which the monks performed their daily tasks, and the space exudes a tranquil and restrained spirituality.

Below: On a table in the elegant *Sala degli Imperatori* stands a modern stone sculpture representing motherhood, a work by Carlo Sassi.

it into a church (known since then as San Nicolò a Maggiano) and selling off the monks' cells and other buildings. And because people in the past lacked the architectural sensibilities displayed today, during the mid nineteenth century the seventeen monks' cells ranged around the great cloister were destroyed without a second thought.

Restoration work, under the personal supervision of Signora Anna Grossi Recordati, has once again revealed the clear, clean lines of the cloister, with its paving of small bricks and its central well that acts as a fulcrum for the four sides of the square. For the restoration of the interior she called upon the services of a specialist in the field, the architect Enzo Mongiardino, who emerged from the project satisfied but exhausted from his endeavours.

The splendid *Sala degli Imperatori* is

first room to greet the visitor. It owes its name to the twelve eighteenth-century Venetian canvases depicting various Roman emperors, who are portrayed on horses in full ceremonial array, displaying that arrogant disdain only the all-powerful possess. The idea for this decor came from Mongiardino, who, in collaboration with the owners, chose almost all the furnishings for the various rooms. There is a very fine piece of seventeenth-century Venetian furniture with beautifully carved drawers, while the wooden spheres adorning the tables, which were painted by the architect himself, make an attractive decorative feature. There is also a remarkable stone carving, *La Maternità*, the work of Carlo Sassi, a respected sculptor who is also a heart surgeon and a friend and former assistant of Professor Grossi. The reading room, surrounded by an architectural bookcase in alder wood, is an interpretation by Mongiardino of the nineteenth-century English style. Mongiardino was also responsible for designing the beautiful walnut sofas with their striped silk upholstery in shades of red, brown and blue, commissioned from a Florentine silk manufacturer who specializes in such fabrics.

The adjacent games room, which contains two tables bearing chessboards complete with chessmen, also bears the stamp of the architect in the simple wicker chairs and the small alder wood tables.

Above: This charming nineteenth-century porcelain coffee service is signed Richard Ginori.

Opposite: Mongiardino has also made his mark on the dining room with two striking items of furniture: a large, decorative display cabinet; and a sideboard surmounted by a classical-style mirror. Both appear to be made of marble, but they are actually painted wood. The plates, painted by various artists, add a colourful warmth.

Below: A closer look at the sideboard in the dining room reveals the high quality of its craftsmanship.

The dining room is particularly attractive; although small it is rich in decorative features, such as the seven tables with their painted wickerwork chairs and an almost theatrical piece of furniture with *faux marbre* decoration inspired by antique models. This contains a collection of some forty plates and dishes painted by different artists who have used their skill with colours to create something more than a mere dinner service. The same piece of furniture also displays a nineteenth-century Richard Ginori coffee service, which is remarkable both for the quality of its porcelain and for the fact that each cup bears the hand-painted symbol of the various *contrade* that take part in the Palio at Siena. There is the lumbering tortoise, the mythical unicorn, the snail, the owl, the porcupine. A fine painting with a rural subject of the seventeenth-century Tuscan school rounds off the room, giving it a feeling of elegance that underlines the importance of hospitality and of gastronomic enjoyment.

The park surrounding the Certosa is dotted with such features as a vineyard, an orchard and a kitchen garden, just as it was during the time of the monks. This is a place of silence, the first Carthusian monastery to take root in Tuscan soil, the first building to bear witness to a religious spirit that at the time was a novelty, but never an abstraction. And visitors today can still sense its special mood.

CHIESINA DI MONTAUTO

The tiny, ancient church of Montauto has stood for more than a thousand years. The countryside around it is still the same one that surrounded it many centuries ago: a bare, pale brown landscape, the clay soil of Siena, where knots of sheep amble slowly like soft clouds over the brows of hills.

The church rests on the very top of a hill, almost a small mountain, which rises above the other hills. At a distance, however, it is invisible, hidden behind a clump of cypresses that stand out in this landscape almost totally bereft of greenery.

Due to dwindling congregations the church was deconsecrated many years ago, and today it is home to a French artist. But if it is true that art nourishes the spirit in the same way as prayer, then the change cannot have been too much of an upheaval for this sacred building. Gerard Fromanger, French by birth but Tuscan by adoption, is a man deeply involved in life, interested in all that happens around him, blessed with a critical eye and a gift for intelligent argument, characteristics reflected in his work. He spends many months in Paris, but whenever he feels tired he travels to Montauto,

Above: A lunette above the entrance to the church contains this tondo of the Virgin and Child, a decorative element that recalls the building's former role.

Opposite: Gerard Fromanger's studio reflects the artist's fertile intellectual and creative life. Here, within the walls of the church, he can find peace and solitude. A short avenue of cypresses leads up to the church, whose small rose window beneath the fine beamed ceiling floods the interior with light.

unpacks his luggage, goes outside to breathe in the fresh sparkling air, and then spends much of the day closeted in the nave of the church. It is here that he works: where once there was an altar, pews for the faithful and sacred images there are now trestle tables and a long stage on which to rest canvases, tubes of paint and brushes. Covered by a fine, pale-coloured beamed ceiling that softens the stark contours of the nave, the room has lost none of its spiritual dimension.

Gerard Fromanger often shuts himself away in his studio. His inspiration is as lively here as it is in Paris, but the brightness and clarity of the Tuscan landscape and the gentle, disquieting nature of its countryside set a particular mood. Perhaps, enclosed in the nave of the church, he is even more alone, even more completely an artist.

When Fromanger bought the church he embarked, with the help of several master masons, on a careful programme of restoration that was effectively a rescue operation. But that tiny church, later to become his studio, concealed a secret or, perhaps more correctly, a treasure. Not the sort of treasure to make a man rich, but something much more precious and

more evocative, something that strengthens one's attachment to a place. In a wall of the nave a large package was discovered, wrapped in old newspaper. But it was not, as one might think, the life savings of some parish priest who had hidden his worldy wealth away for safekeeping, although the protagonist of the story was indeed a priest, Don Francesco Canaletti, curate of Montauto for some fifty years. The package was found to contain a five-hundred page manuscript, a poem of more than ten thousand lines, in which the priest railed bitterly against the many people who had wronged him. After the artist had read it through he felt great sympathy and affection for that priest who had lived at the beginning of this century; it may even have been the reason he

Far left: The small belfry plays host to a cypress sapling.

Left and below: A distant view of the artist's home, formerly the priest's house, which clings to the side of the church (below). The entire group of buildings is made of brick.

chose the church as the center of his creative activities.

The slender facade, made completely of brick, is pierced by a small rose window that floods the interior with light, and the two buildings at either side of the church are also made of the same material. A small and unusual double-sided belfry has given sanctuary to the seed from a cypress, which has sprouted between the stones and is now a small tree.

Left: The entrance features these brick arches in the Sienese taste which may once have formed a shallow external portico.

Opposite: The study–sitting room carries on the natural, unforced style chosen by Gerard Fromanger. Perched on a hill amid an undulating, almost featureless landscape, these buildings were once a church and home to a priest. The interiors were designed to reflect a feeling of sober essentiality, with no concessions to frivolous indulgence.

Although it obviously cannot stay there, for the moment its slender trunk projects a feeling of wildness and freedom. The entrance derives a perspective quality from its brick arches, which may once have been open to the light, acting as a sort of small portico.

The simple kitchen opens into a beautiful sitting room that is used for parties; it contains a fine brick fireplace covered by an age-old beam. The artist's study reflects the same feeling of simplicity, with no unnecessary decorative refinements: a soft and welcoming sofa, a large number of books arranged on functional bookshelves, an old rustic Tuscan table of the late nineteenth century and a bentwood rocking chair in which Gerard Fromanger can relax and gather his thoughts. Everything is in keeping with the spirit of the owner, who did not acquire this religious building to turn it into something different, to empty it of its spiritual content or demean it with ostentations or insensitive furnishings. There is a great deal of respect in this simple furniture and real love and understanding in the decision by the church's lay guardian to make only the minimum of changes to its thousand-year-old fabric.

CASTLES

Castles not only excite the imagination of children, they appeal to adults as well. In many areas of Tuscany, castles perch high atop hills and mountains overlooking lush green fields and forests. Inaccessible and impregnable, they dominate the countryside like solitary, indestructible giants.

CASTELLO DI BROLIO

Long rows of vines create random geometric patterns punctuated by paths cut into the soil. It is a rustic landscape of contrasts: the colours of the vineyards and olive groves are warm and gentle while the cypresses are dark and somber, their tall, nervous shapes marking the progress of tracks and roadways as they sprout skyward like sentinels on the horizon. It is a landscape whose completely natural appearance conceals centuries of hard work and loving care, a mosaic created by sober, artful minds. This is the countryside of Chianti, one of the most beautiful spots in the area of Gaiole in the province of Siena. And it is on a small hill in this district that the massive ramparts of the Castello di Brolio have stood for hundreds of years. A group of buildings that seems to have sprung from the imagination, it is, in fact, the product of various periods and styles that blends perfectly into the landscape.

At a distance it looks like some brick and stone giant, with typically lofty Tuscan trees springing from its entrails. The stone belongs to the ramparts and the ancient structures contained within them, while all the bricks, sometimes dark red and sometimes paler, belong to

Above: Through one of the many neo-Gothic windows on the upper floor comes this glimpse of the Chianti countryside, a landscape of pale, softly changing colours, on which humans have made their mark without destroying its original appearance.

Opposite: The elegant entrance hall, with its sweeping arches atop slender Ionic columns, was part of the nineteenth-century alterations. The stone staircase leading to the upper floors displays an attractive series of balusters that are also in the Ionic style. The whole area is covered by a wooden ceiling whose decorative details are picked out in gold. The terra-cotta stand still contains the walking sticks and canes belonging to recent ancestors of the family.

the main body of the castle. This part is much more recent in date and was inspired by the ancient architecture of Siena, whose elegant skyline can almost be sensed on the horizon. The mixture of architectural styles is dominated by the warlike quality still exuded by the walls and the keep, a feeling of aggression reflected in a mood of rugged, uncompromising solidity. This is counterbalanced by the strongly evocative feeling, both intellectual and emtional, radiated by the central body of the complex, which was extensively altered in the neo-Gothic style during the nineteenth century by the Sienese architect Pietro Marchetti, who refaced the castle's ancient walls in brick. This new covering, which at times fits rather uneasily with the earlier architectural features, has now become perfectly integrated, creating a strong, theatrical effect.

Baron Bettino Ricasoli, whose family has owned Brolio since the dawn of the millennium, directs the famous winery that bears the castle's name and which has now been moved to the slopes of the hill. His aristocratic face betrays centuries of noble breeding. It is also an unmistakeably Tuscan face, which bears the

Above: The central part of the Castello di Brolio, in the neo-Gothic style, has mullioned lancet windows and balconies with finely decorated corbels. It is clad entirely in brick, a choice dictated by the desire to maintain a sense of stylistic coherence with the ancient buildings of nearby Siena.

Above right: Within the walls stand two beautiful architectural features. The small family chapel, whose roof is seen in the foreground, dates back to the fourteenth century and contains the tombs of several famous Ricasoli, including the Iron Baron. In the background rises the stark outline of the medieval keep, which once gave refuge to the castle's inhabitants when enemies penetrated the outer walls.

Left: The castle's merlons are visible from far away. The solid ring of walls, once a bulwark against attacks by enemy horsemen, rests on the crest of the hill like a sleeping giant. Around it lies a dense network of vines.

mark of such illustrious ancestors as his namesake and great-grandfather, who contributed to the birth of a united Italy; the famous "Iron Baron" who succeeded Cavour as prime minister after the unification. This is also the Bettino Ricasoli regarded by many as the man who created, or rather classified, Chianti Classico, one of the world's most famous wines. The present Bettino Ricasoli is a gracious host who regales visitors to his vast property with tales of its tumultuous history.

The name of the place derives from the Germanic word *broilo* (orchard) which betrays the presence of a Lombard settlement in the area. The first documentary evidence of the castle dates from 1004. In 1176, after the imperial defeat at Legnano, the Florentines expanded their frontiers, depriving the Sienese of, among

other things, the Castello di Brolio. Siena tried for many years to regain its outpost at Brolio, but to no avail, and even bands of bloodthirsty adventurers tried in vain to storm the stronghold. In 1432, however, its walls were successfully breached by Antonio Petrucci, a Sienese soldier of fortune. According to the

Above: Another splendid entrance hall contains a seventeenth-century Tuscan chest and a beautiful hanging embroidered with the coat of arms of the ancient Ricasoli family.

Opposite: In the lofty *salone delle armi* everything seems to reflect the castle's aggressive, warlike origins: the monastic-style table, the suits of armour, the family standards and the stone fireplace.

chronicles, this man succeeded in penetrating the closely guarded complex by means of a brilliant act of daring, the speed of which caught the sentries completely unawares. Brolio suddenly fell to the Sienese, although it was almost as rapidly retaken by the Florentines. Antonio Petrucci, who was taken prisoner, fell into disgrace.

In 1452, Duke Ferdinando of Calabria, son of the king of Naples, made an unsuccessful assault on the castle with his Aragonese soldiers. In 1478, another attack was launched by Aragonese troops, who on this occasion managed to recapture the castle so it was returned to the Sienese. Because in those days there was no thought of preserving such monuments for posterity, the Sienese embarked on the total demolition of the castle, perhaps to punish it for having been in the hands of the hated Florentines for so long. Shortly afterwards, the pendulum swung back again and, thanks to the peace treaty drawn up by Lorenzo de' Medici, it was returned to Florence. It was during this period that the castle was given a new set of walls (the ones that can be seen today), which were probably built after 1484 by Giuliano da Sangallo, one of the greatest architects in the service of the Medici. But Brolio was yet again to fall victim to the perennial rivalry between Florence and Siena.

In 1529, it fell to a band of Spanish

Opposite: The light flooding through the windows seems to intensify the colours of this room's decor. A very finely worked antique carpet covers almost the entire floor, and the room is dotted with porcelain and majolica pieces and with chairs and tables in the neo-Gothic taste. But the most striking features are the wall decorations, which have a stamped-leather covering of clearly Spanish inspiration, and the coffered wooden ceiling, a regal covering for an equally regal *salotto* whose breathtaking surroundings inspire a feeling of respect and even awe. This is one of those sumptuous, richly decorated rooms that stays in the memory.

Right above: This charming terra-cotta tondo in the castello, which shows a circle of cherubs paying homage to the Virgin and Child, represents a touching iconographical image that appears frequently in traditional Tuscan tondos. This tradition became established in Tuscany thanks to the genius of Luca, Andrea and Giovanni Della Robbia, who created works of extraordinary aesthetic quality and very moving expressiveness. The Madonnas produced by the Della Robbia family were the result of a special technical process – still only partly understood – based on polychrome, tin-glazed enamels that increased the plastic qualities of the figures. The tondo seen here is derived from these fifteenth-century masterpieces.

Right below: The Ricasoli Firidolfi coat of arms can still be seen on the walls of many old castles in Chianti, which was once a family fief. Today it also appears on the many bottles of wine produced at the castello, recalling the time when, in 1847, Baron Ricasoli devised the blend of grapes to be used in the making of Chianti Classico.

mercenaries in the service of the imperial army, but, following the restoration of the Medici, it was recaptured by Florence. From that moment on Brolio would remain under Florentine control, acting as a look-out, an outpost of Florentine power, a strong and faithful sentry guarding the frontiers of the city's territory.

As we pass through the great entrance in the company of the baron, the atmosphere is suddenly different: the air is still and motionless and we are surrounded by the spirits of the past. It is as though a secret life were slowly unfolding, grudgingly revealing its mysteries, a life written indelibly in the stones and in the countless tales that are still handed down in these parts, the sort of tales that surround any real castle. But there is more to Brolio than mere legend. There is the fascinating family chapel, dating back to 1348, whose facade is decorated with a relatively modern yet unobtrusive mosaic; the nearby structure of the medieval keep, with its solid towers, which once gave refuge to the inhabitants of the castle in the event of the walls being breached; and the reassuringly solid walls, on average some 15 meters (50 feet) high, which surround the castle for a distance of 450 meters (1,465 feet). It is possible to look up at these imposing walls from the old communication trenches and from the gently winding paths of the great park, which is in the nineteenth-century taste.

There is also the restrained elegance of the small Italian garden, a pattern of symmetrical box hedges clipped into different geometric shapes. Above all, however, there is the neo-Gothic palazzo, whose facade displays a series of three-mullioned lancets and balconies supported by finely decorated corbels. Its interior is an endless maze of rooms, many of which were refurbished by Marchetti in keeping with the neo-Gothic taste of the exterior. Even though some areas have been embellished with rather heavy decoration, the overall scheme has a precise intellectual intent: to pay homage to the spirit of the Middle Ages and to the castle's severe and sober past. The result is a spacious dining room adorned with standards, suits of armour and a simple table designed personally by the architect, with walls richly decorated in the medieval style. But two of the most impressive of the castle's many rooms are the "red *salotto*" and the "green room," both of which have retained their original fifteenth-century appearance. They share the same uncluttered lines and the same feeling of simplicity, their only concession to decoration being the wooden cross vaults of their ceilings, which display a dense tracery of carving.

There is also a splendid library, a treasure house of books, many of them centuries old, as well as an archive of family documents, some of which have yet to be

Above: The library of the castello is a vast treasure house of ancient volumes and centuries-old documents, some of which have yet to be properly studied and catalogued. These papers contain the whole history of the castle, as well as that of the Chianti countryside, the countless villages that dot its territory and the endless battles that once raged among these hills. The library also contains a mute presence, the portrait of the man who contributed so much to it, Baron Bettino Ricasoli, one of the protagonists in the Unification of Italy.

Opposite: This is the favourite room of many of the Ricasoli. In keeping with the typically austere taste of Tuscany, it displays almost no unnecessary luxury. The walls are bare of decoration, the ceiling retains its simple vaulting, and the whole thing possesses a serenely spiritual mood. It is, in fact, one of the few rooms to have escaped the alterations carried out during the nineteenth century and remains a jewel of thirteenth–fourteenth-century architecture.

deciphered. A portrait of the stern, unyielding face of the Iron Baron looks down over the vast array of books, almost as though he were standing guard.

There is not enough space here to go into a detailed description of the countless tapestries scattered through the different rooms, the period furniture, the precious porcelain and majolica. These are all reminders of the many generations of Ricasoli who spent the greater part of their lives here, behind the walls of this gilded fortress, this castle that is also a home, very much alive and busy.

Bettino Ricasoli spends his working life at Brolio, where he runs a large wine-making enterprise, with 25 hectares (62 acres) of flourishing vineyards that yield ten million bottles a year. It is the largest winery in Chianti and certainly the most glorious and historic one: as early as the seventeenth century large oak casks were leaving Brolio, filled with wine to grace the lavish banquets of feudal lords throughout Europe; and, during the second part of the nineteenth century, it was the Iron Baron who codified the rules governing the production of Chianti Classico. Today, the winery produces a variety of different wines, the most distinguished of which bear the "Brolio" label and the "Ricasoli" label. New wines have also been introduced as part of a process of experimentation and expansion and to meet the demands of the market.

CASTELLO DI MELETO

The two solid turrets have stood guard for centuries. They come into view at the start of a narrow, gently climbing road, then they vanish, only to reappear round a bend, outlined by shafts of light filtered through a wooded maze of cypresses and limes. The Castello di Meleto is sunk in silence, the owner's car the only discordant element of a scene rooted in bygone days that here still seem to survive, feeding on the lingering echoes of ages passed. Meleto dates from the Middle Ages, from the days of Count Ugo, marchese of Tuscany, who in 970 gave these lands and their original buildings (at that time much smaller and more primitive) to the Vallombrosan Benedictine monks of the Badia a Coltibuono.

The castle stands in the Sienese area of Chianti, in the *comune* of Gaiole, considered Tuscany's answer to the Loire valley, and it is one of the most interesting groups of fortified buildings in the region. The nucleus of the castle with its great square keep, which is now surrounded by later structures, was built during the thirteenth century. The lords of the region during this period were the Ricasoli Firidolfi, relations of the Ranieri who, so the history books

Above: A shaded glimpse of the castello. In the foreground stands the proud fifteenth-century turret that, with its twin (seen in the background), was erected to make the earlier structure even more impregnable.

Opposite: A bird's-eye view shows the sturdy proportions of Meleto, with its two fifteenth-century turrets and, at the center, its medieval keep. The seventeenth-century facade, which is in the shade, leads on to a green "terrace" overlooking the surrounding countryside. In front of the main facade, which is framed by the two turrets, it is possible to make out the shapes of a few small houses. They are all that remains of the old village and were once the humble dwellings of the serfs who worked the estate in the service of their feudal lord.

tell us, was on very good terms with Emperor Frederick Barbarossa. As time went by, Meleto was so extensively enlarged that by the fifteenth century it already possessed its two massive turrets and was very similar, at least in its external appearance, to the castle we see today. In 1478, it was captured from the Florentines by the Sienese with the help of troops in the service of the Aragonese king of Naples, who inflicted severe damage on it. The Florentines recaptured it, however, and, despite further attempts to retake it, it remained firmly in Florentine hands, later becoming part of the Grand Duchy of Tuscany. This marked the end of the castle's turbulent life: the attacks on its walls, the violent assaults, the glint of armour, the cries of encouragement and fear, the splashes of blood and sweat were now nothing more than a glorious and tragic memory. The role of the fortress changed and, after 1738, it was turned into a villa by its owner at the time, senator Ricasoli Zanchini. He made a number of alterations to the western facade and to the interior, which was adorned with light-hearted decorations and wall paintings extolling the pleasures of the rustic life, and fitted with spacious

Far left: An attractive ornamental detail of the miniature eighteenth-century theater set up for the entertainment of the owners and their close circle of friends.

Left: This brightly coloured decoration dates from the period when the castello was transformed from an austere, warlike fortress into a pleasant country residence.

Below: The rooms on the *piano nobile* lead into one another in an unbroken line, as in this dynamic perspective view which seems to stretch into infinity.

rooms that reflected the owner's wealth and breeding.

The castello lost part of its rough and ready charm. The communication trenches, the armouries, the countless trapdoors and secret passages all disappeared. But the stories survived, the often chilling tales both real and imagined, recounted by local people. Sinister legends like the one concerning the skull found during restoration work in the eighteenth century that still retained a pair of piercing black eyes and which turned to dust when blessed. Or the story about the weapons and human bones discovered at the bottom of a well, probably the remains of some hapless Sienese assailants who were captured and summarily executed by the Florentines. Stories of this sort, however, do not detract from the charm of such buildings, if anything they add to it, since castles are by their very nature filled with a feeling of

Right: A detail of one of the many doors adorned with flowers, leaves and greenery. Once the castello had become a peaceful country home, such decorative references to its natural surroundings were almost obligatory.

Below: In the dining room, which is entirely in the eighteenth-century style, the elegant fireplace is crowned by a stucco decoration reproducing the coat of arms of the owners at the time. The chairs, which are probably contemporary with the general decoration of the room, make a particularly interesting feature.

adventure and mystery, a sense of the turbulence of history.

The exterior of Meleto is a happy marriage of different centuries: the broad central keep, the oldest element, almost hidden by the surrounding walls; the eastern face, also of great age, made of medieval masonry in solid, rusticated stone whose projections are now barely visible; the western facade, altered between the seventeenth and eighteenth centuries, with its six large windows opening into the *piano nobile* and a noble doorway surrounded by elegant stucco work; and finally, the main facade, whose steep walls are encased between the two fifteenth-century turrets that announce their presence from many miles away.

Remo Ciampi cares for the castello with great respect, accompanying visitors around the interior of his property, which is not the only one in the area, with a feeling of understandable satisfaction. The interior is a delightful discovery: a cross between a private house and an antiquarian collection, it combines a feeling of human warmth with the impressive atmosphere of a museum. Despite the fact that many of the walls date from medieval times, the rooms have eighteenth-century decorations that are so light and airy they seem almost to float, while the elegantly descriptive frescoes create a feeling of serenity.

Left: No one has slept in this eighteenth-century bed with its snow-white canopy for many years. Everything in this room appears to be frozen in time, suspended between the present and the past. The wall displays an impressive painting in which the dark trees in the foreground contrast with the warm light bathing the ships and towers in the distance.

Opposite: The airiness and elegance of the reception room is enhanced by the pale colours of the ceiling and the large, delicately painted mural over the fireplace.

Below: On each side of the altar in the small chapel, located next to the reception room, stands a seventeenth-century candelabra in the form of an angel, radiating a mood of timeless serenity.

The rooms, which run around the perimeter of the castle, are filled with surprises. Set into the wall of one room, for example, is a small, ancient archive containing a number of old books and documents covering three hundred years of daily life, while another room displays a portrait depicting the haughty, regal features of Giangastone de' Medici, Grand Duke of Tuscany, with his proud eyes, hooked nose, and shoulder-length hair.

The long, narrow dining room with its table of similar dimensions, contains a portrait of a kindly figure who seems to have emerged from one of the tales of the Brothers Grimm. It is, in fact, a likeness of the architect who transformed the castello's interior in 1738; his expression suggests that he was quite rightly pleased with the work he carried out with such precision and dedication.

A step into another room takes us back

in time, where high on the wall hangs a fresco removed from a neighbouring church. It depicts the delicate features of an enthroned Madonna with her curly-headed Child and saints. It is the work of an unknown master of the early fifteenth century who probably trained in Florence. Beneath this fresco stands a small display cabinet containing a number of ecclesiastical objects and church vestments that would be the joy of any connoisseur of the decorative arts.

A short distance away is a magnificent canopied bed in an enchanting bedroom whose walls are decorated with a large canvas showing groups of trees in the foreground with a distant view of ships and towers in the background. The most remarkable room, however, is probably the vast sitting room, once reserved for receptions; the elaborately decorative ceiling and frieze complement the narrative quality of the two murals that face each other across the room. The most striking of these two views portrays a classical architectural landscape in which a woman crosses a stretch of water, desperately clutching her struggling child.

The nearby private chapel, a place of worship and silence, possesses a fine late-sixteenth century Madonna and Child on the altar, while, at either side, the serene faces and gold robes of the two wooden angels supporting candelabras give an ethereal feeling to their surroundings.

The upper floor is of less importance, though it is set within an enclosed loggia off which lead many high-ceilinged rooms.

From the small courtyard, which is enclosed by walls but open to the sky, a simple door leads unexpectedly into a tiny theater, perfect in every detail and equipped with everything needed to put on a play. For as long as anyone can remember it has remained unused, but for many years it represented a cultural pastime for countless owners of Meleto.

Beneath the *piano nobile*, and running around the entire perimeter of the castle, stand the great cellars, which for centuries were used to store and age the Chianti wines that have brought worldwide fame to so many ancient residences. Meleto boasts an excellent wine, dark red in colour, with a full bouquet and a high alcoholic content. It is a carefully nurtured

Preceding spread: The vineyards of Tuscany are one of its most characteristic features. The trellises of skilfully trained vines produce some of the world's most famous wines.

Opposite: It looks like a stage set or a puppet theater, as if at any moment actors or marionettes might suddenly make an appearance. But off to the right, one catches a giveaway glimpse of a tub – this is the bathroom on the *piano nobile*, enveloped in the luminous greens of an idealized painted countryside.

Below: On this seventeenth-century Tuscan chest the highly imaginative architect who modernized the castello outlined the plans for his alterations, which unfortunately were never fully realized. The chest has thus become a precious piece of documentary evidence, not preserved in some dusty archive but readily viewed by all. Note the keyhole cleverly disguised as one of the window openings.

Above: The curtain of the tiny eighteenth-century theater depicts the planned and only partly finished alterations, just like the chest that stands in the *piano nobile*. The architect's descriptive talents were such that this picture is not just a valuable document, but also a work of art of some importance.

wine, a fine Chianti Classico, and a source of great pride for Remo Ciampi, who each year produces some two million bottles of it.

Ciampi, a Florentine to the core, discovered Chianti in 1960 when everyone was leaving the countryside, and people thought that farming had entered a period of irreversible decline. He bought a number of properties in the area, including Meleto, and time has proved how right his instincts as a businessman were. Meleto also produces an excellent white wine and a fine dessert wine; other labels are also planned.

The business, now a truly vast enterprise, continues to hold high the traditions of a wine that has for many centuries been produced in a strictly authentic way. It is this authenticity that Ciampi holds most dear, because he regards his wine making as more than just a commercial undertaking. For Ciampi, wine is the distinguishing feature of these ancient lands and he regards himself as more than just an enthusiast and a connoisseur. The Castello di Meleto and the classic Chianti wines from its hills represent the true spirit of Tuscany.

But gradually, as the turrets disappear, the asphalt road resumes, and with it, the hubbub of modern life. Meleto, with its knights and the shadows of its living past, remains suspended in its mood of timeless silence.

CASTELLO DI VOLPAIA

Giovanna Stianti, a young, elegant Florentine lady is the enthusiastic chatelaine of a magnificent castle. The splendidly rustic Castello di Volpaia is a fortified stronghold of medieval origins. It has everything: a solid, square-shaped keep, the remains of the old walls, the narrow, cramped alleys through which the life-blood of the community flows, an old well, an even more ancient spring and a few small churches hidden among the houses. The odd car drives past; nearby is a small café that also acts as a general store, whose owner, during closing hours, looks after her hens and sells fresh eggs.

It seems impossible, but at Volpaia the glories of the past still exist and even blend in with the realities of modern life. Volpaia does not cling to its origins, it is not trapped in gilded oblivion without a present: it still lives the busy life of a hill town whose people have made a decision to remain apart from the mainstream, but not to disappear altogether. A strong and friendly community spirit is at work here.

Giovanna Stianti, known to everyone as Giovannella, owns a great many of the houses at Volpaia and divides her life between the town and the very different environment of Milan, where her family is

Above: Many of the houses' facades display sacred images that accompany the visitors and residents through the narrow streets and alleyways of the town, an invitation to serenity and contemplation.

Opposite: The buildings of the fortified hilltown of Volpaia appear to sink into the green countryside. Looking at the cluster of houses, the bell tower of the old church and the ancient keep, the modern visitor can sense that this is a farming community, a place where men and women work the soil. Life here used to be very different, however, when medieval walls enclosed the town and the place bristled with armed men. The Castello di Volpaia was one of the many strongholds belonging to Florence, a city to which it always remained loyal, even though it was breached by the Sienese on more than one occasion.

based. She is also well known in Tuscany as a wine producer.

Signora Stianti is Volpaia's latest owner, but it is hard to establish who was its first. A document dated April 21, 1172, mentions the castello, when the two owners, the brothers Franculus and Galfredus da Cintoia, having obtained the consent of their father and of "Liquiritia, wife of Franculus," used the properties as a pledge against a loan of 38 *libbre* from one Spinello da Montegrossoli, who may have been a moneylender. These properties were situated "within the court and castle at Vulpaio." But at that time the fortified town had already stood for at least two centuries. It was an area that would later become a battleground between the Sienese and the Florentines, who on more than one occasion conquered and reconquered the town in an ebb and flow of military fortunes that did not end until 1480, when a truce was finally signed between the two proud and powerful adversaries. The castello now took on a completely agricultural role, and with considerable success, judging by the houses that were built with fine late Renaissance doorways, sometimes incorporating parts of the medieval walls. As

Left: A glimpse of the small garden belonging to Signora Giovanna Stianti. The grass spills over the smooth paving stones, while the terra-cotta pots of lemon trees are a feature no self-respecting Tuscan country home would be without. In the background stand some of the small houses of the town and a remarkable church, now deconsecrated, which was inspired by the work of Michelozzi.

Below left: A view of the town's rugged architecture.

Below right: The owners' garden is rather like a terrace overlooking the Chianti countryside. It contains these two ancient millstones, once driven by mules, as a sort of homage to manual labour.

Opposite: The keep, whose massive structure dominates the town, contains the wine cellars of the Fattoria Castello di Volpaia. It is here that the wines are skilfully aged before being exported all over the world. These serried ranks of bottles project a much more convivial feeling than the ranks of armed men who once inhabited the keep.

was the case with many historic Chianti residences, the main focus was on wine growing.

Today, the lofty keep houses sophisticated cellars where the wine is aged and which also act as refreshment rooms for the many visitors eager to sample this noble, robust Tuscan wine. Shortly after the keep we come to an attractive room whose decorated doorway gives it a

Around the nearby well stands the fifteenth-century church, deconsecrated in 1932, whose architectural design reflects the influence of Michelozzi, and the home of the owners, which, although of more recent construction, is equally attractive. A small garden acts as a terrace over the surrounding Chianti countryside and its many rooms reflect the sober yet fanciful nature of its proprietors. In fact, no sooner have visitors entered the building than they get the feeling they are looking out over the sea, here in the middle of the countryside.

One wall contains a recent decorative addition in the form of a highly attractive painted lunette. The artist responsible for this very affectionate work is Luciano Guarnieri, known throughout the world for his skilful brushwork and particularly for his portraits. The lunette depicts Giovannella Stianti in the company of her young son. To enhance the unique atmosphere of this room a long, horseshoe-shaped sofa runs round the walls.

Although the castello has many rooms, it is almost as though the whole interior were one large space. The dining room, for example – with its refectory table and brass lamp that would be at home on board ship – features an arch leading into other rooms. There is another door that opens up into the kitchen, which is preceded by a corridor adorned with a riot of leaves, flowers and – in a highly original

certain elegance. The interior has the clean, reassuring appearance of an old pharmacy or herbalist's shop. It is, however, the workshop of the resident oenologist who, with a team of assistants, carefully supervises the development of the latest vintage, experimenting, tasting and blending, just like an alchemist of old, but using the latest methods and high-technology equipment.

Above: The entrance is decorated with rustic floral motifs. The door in the background leads into the spacious kitchen.

Opposite: The dining room, embraced by a solid arch, possesses a wooden ceiling with massive beams and the traditional Tuscan brick floor. On the table, lit by an elaborate brass lamp, are two bottles of Chianti Classico Castello di Volpaia, one of the most sought-after labels.

touch – insects. This decorative scheme was painted by a master restorer from Siena, who, at the request of the owner, let his imagination run riot. The tiny insects, which include spiders and their webs, have been painted on the walls with a meticulous attention to detail, a feeling of freshness and realism and in an almost childlike spirit of observation. Among the many interesting rooms on the upper floor is a *salotto* containing several important pieces displayed in a completely natural, unaffected manner, such as the large walnut bookcase enclosed within three columns and the splendid eighteenth-century Venetian chandelier.

The small town of Volpaia is characterized by peace and quiet. On leaving, visitors vow to return as soon as possible because Volpaia welcomes them in a completely unforced way, putting them at their ease and displaying that typically Tuscan style of informal hospitality.

Volpaia is also home to a very gracious wine, Chianti Classico Castello di Volpaia, which is ruby red with bright amber shades, an exceptionally intense, lingering bouquet, and a dry, well-rounded taste. It is almost a declaration of love, but it is a fully requited love because this label, known to the world's finest palates, is truly synonymous with fine wine. And the single-minded philsophy of the owners is to strive constantly for quality. The Volpaia estate covers 333 hectares (823

Above: The upper floor of the owners' house contains a *salotto*, whose features include a fine walnut bookcase and a particularly splendid eighteenth-century chandelier, made by the skilful hands of Venetian craftsmen.

Opposite: This underground passage links the castello to the keep.

Below: This wall displays a lunette-shaped painting by Luciano Guarnieri depicting Giovannella Stianti with her young son.

acres), but only 30 hectares (74 acres) of these are planted with specialized vines because, after careful research, it was decided to establish vineyards only on the best land, the dry, south-facing areas. The Azienda Castello di Volpaia may, however, have faced more difficulties than any other Chianti vineyard. In 1972, for example, after the harvest had been deemed unsatisfactory, the entire crop was sold to other wineries and no wine from Volpaia was put on the market. It was thought better to suffer financially than to forfeit the respect of the connoisseurs, who are the most demanding customers and also the people who do the most to spread the reputation of a wine.

At Volpaia they not only make a great wine, but from it they demand a special taste and a unique bouquet. They work to create a product that will do full justice to a whole tradition, culture and way of life.

CASTELLO DI GARGONZA

From the top of the castellated tower the cluster of roofs seems to join together in a solid, unbroken mass, while a gentle tide of red tiles follows irregular lines. The effect is so cramped that the tiles seem to be in danger of spilling on to the ground. This bird's-eye view gives an accurate picture of this microcosm, whose layout is as magical as its modern conversion into residential units is imaginative and practical.

In the sunny silence, accompanied by the owner, conte Roberto Guicciardini Corsi Salviati, we make an open-air tour of the low walls that jealously guard the whole town, with its turreted keep, its beautiful small church, its rare, arched bell tower and its houses, some noble and some more modest, but all of them now containing beautifully appointed apartments much in demand among those seeking peace and quiet in a unique setting.

But what we see is only a part of the remote Castello di Gargonza, once the property of the Ubertini family and later a pawn in the bitter struggle between Guelphs and Ghibellines. It was first occupied by Arretine troops, allies of the Ghibellines under the command of Bishop Guglielmo of Arezzo, who, despite

Above: This glimpse of the fortified hill town of Gargonza captures its mood of total serenity. The simple facade of the small church dedicted to Saints Tiburzio and Susanna is a fine example of country church architecture.

Opposite: An aerial view of the castello, with its cluster of houses divided by narrow alleyways and small streets, encircled by the dense foliage of cypresses and chestnut trees. Even from this angle, the dominant feature is the keep, the oldest structure in the complex, which seems almost to be protecting the inhabitants, still betraying its original function as a look-out.

his ecclesiastical vestments, seems to have been keener on battle and political intrigue than the simple life of Christian humility. In this way Gargonza became part of the Ghibelline domains, and in 1304 it became the scene of a meeting between the Ghibellines of Arezzo and White Guelph fugitives from Florence, one of whom appears to have been the poet Dante himself. In 1307 the noble story of Gargonza almost came to an ignominious end, when the massed armies of Florence moved against Arezzo and the castles of the Ubertini. The Florentines were stronger and more numerous, but the cunning of the Arretines compensated for this disparity in forces. A rumour was circulated that the well-trained cavalry of Cardinal Orsini had in the meantime left Arezzo and was heading for Florence, which had been left under the protection of a mere handful of men. The Florentine troops turned back and hastened to the defense of their city, thus saving Gargonza and many other strongholds and ensuring victory for the Arretines.

During the fourteenth century the castello was sold for a large sum of money to the Sienese, who later ceded it to the

Left: This fine belfry on the roof of the church is an interesting example of its type. Its two small arches contain the bronze bells that call the residents of Gargonza to Mass once a week.

Below left: After passing through the main entrance arch, visitors find themselves facing the small square with its ancient well, from where the narrow streets branch off in a circular pattern. This layout, originally designed for defensive purposes, still retains its old appearance.

Opposite: This is how Gargonza appears to visitors arriving from the village of Monte San Savino. After a brief journey through the countryside, they come to a sunken road that plunges into a shady wood of chestnuts, cypresses and oaks. This picturesque view never fails to make conte Roberto Guicciardini, the owner of the castello, stop in admiration.

Below: Another glimpse of Gargonza. The towered keep with its Guelph merlons dominates every corner of the town.

Florentines. The inhabitants rebelled however, but this time they were obliged to face the full wrath of Florence, which intervened in force and razed the walls of Gargonza to the ground. Its later history was less eventful, and during the eighteenth century the castle and town became the property of the noble Corsi family, who transformed it into a vast agricultural community. In 1833 the town numbered 564 inhabitants.

Today its farming activities are a thing of the past. The peasants who once lived in Gargonza have left, lured away by the doubtful attractions of the city, but their houses still remain. These have now been restored and rented out, still retaining their ancient rural character. The names of their former residents have also survived: there is the unassuming Casa di Nando (Nando's house); the more aristocratic Casa di Palle, heralded by a delightful pergola; the Casa di Bracalino, from which it is possible to gain a splendid view of the keep; the long, low Casa di Lucia; the austere Casa di Nerina; and the houses of the Guardia, the Fattore, and the Famiglia Rossi. This secret, simple, ancient world has survived thanks to the love of Conte Roberto, who as a very small child fell under the spell of Gargonza and became convinced that the town could be saved, without losing any of its original charm, if it were given a new role in life.

The doorway of the little church, dedicated to Saints Tiburzio and Susanna, opens up to reveal a very plain interior with a brick floor and a trussed ceiling. Once a week the priest from the nearby village of Monte San Savino comes here to celebrate Mass for members of a congregation who, although very few in number, are no less devout. There is a very fine

Opposite: The rustic *salotto* provides an anteroom for visitors to the great conference and entertainment hall; it was formerly one of the areas in which the olives were carefully pressed to obtain one of the best oils in the region. The small, simple fireplace, the old wooden beams that appear to support the ceiling and the sprays of broom placed in a large, age-mellowed storage jar, all contribute to a sense of simple yet original informality.

Right: The small houses that wind their way through the town still bear the names of the people who once lived in them so many years ago. Today they provide accommodation for those who holiday in Gargonza. This interior, with its fireplace, rustic walls, beamed ceiling and simple decor, is one of the apartments that once belonged to the few inhabitants of the castello.

Overleaf: This typical view of the Tuscan countryside conveys a feeling both of peace and honest toil.

altar made of travertine, while an arched window with a single mullion in the form of a tiny marble column lets in a shaft of light that illuminates a fragment of a fourteenth-century fresco. Also in the church is a beautiful late-fifteenth-century painting, the property of the Uffizi gallery, depicting the delicate features of a Madonna and Child surrounded by saints and angels. A precious gilded ciborium rests on a small column behind the altar.

The church is still filled with echoes of the religious devotions of Lucia, Nerina, Nando and all the other simple folk of Gargonza, now vanished, whose memory lives on within these walls.

Shortly beyond the church stands the room that once housed the old olive press. Skilfully restored and still retaining elements of the old medieval walls, it now acts as a conference and convention center.

The family apartments of the Guicciardini Corsi Salviati contain a rustic room graced with a finely worked seventeenth-century fireplace, while the remainder of the decor reflects the austere mood of the town. But there is another element to embellish the owners' home: an ancient courtyard that leads into a garden laid out by Giulio Guicciardini Corsi Salviati, father of the present owner. It was conte Giulio, renowned in Florence for his great

learning, who personally designed the garden in the noble Italian tradition. Here, however, the flower beds are not fringed with box hedges, but more simply adorned with a swirling mass of roses in full bloom.

In the background, acting as a boundary to this green space, is an element derived from the old gardens of central Europe: a box hedge interspersed with bushes, also of box, clipped into tall corkscrew shapes. At the side stand typically Tuscan cypresses with their dense green foliage.

On the arch over the gateway to the town an inscription reads: ". . . Dante, sensing his ruin, immediately left Rome, where he was ambassador. Travelling quickly, he came to Siena, where, clearly sensing the calamity that had befallen him and finding no refuge, he decided to join the other fugitives. His first meeting was with a gathering of these fugitives at Gargonza, where he discussed many matters, finally settling in Arezzo . . ." This excerpt from a text written by the nineteenth-century historian Leonardo Bruni heightens Gargonza's sense of history, acting as a further attraction to all those who, unlike Dante, come here to relax.

The Castello di Gargonza is situated 7 kilometers (about 4 miles) from Monte San Savino in the province of Arezzo, set amidst a luxuriant landscape that seems almost to engulf it.

Opposite: The apartments of the Guicciardini Corsi Salviati family contain this fine seventeenth-century fireplace whose simple, unassuming lines are typical of the great fireplaces found in houses throughout the Tuscan countryside.

Above and below: Two views of the small garden, designed in the early twentieth century by Giulio Guicciardini, father of the present owner. The green area has been laid out in the Italian taste, but there are also elements reminiscent of the central European style of garden.

Conte Roberto Guicciardini Corsi Salviati is the man who has put it on the map. In 1972 Gargonza was practically uninhabited and falling into decay. The dilemma facing the conte was whether to leave it to its undeserved fate or bring it back to life under a new identity. He eventually decided to look to England for help and placed an advertisement in *The Times*. The response was immediate and overwhelming: Gargonza would not be allowed to die. Restoration work began and, in a few hectic years, the town was reborn, stone by stone and brick by brick.

The houses were originally rented to artists and writers in search of peace and inspiration. In recent years, however, companies and universities have arrived, organizing congresses, conventions and study groups. Each year the popularity of the castello grows. "It is important to emphasize," says its owner, "how this building, which once seemed to be going into decline, has been taken to people's hearts and brought back to life by the sensibilities of all those who appreciate its secret message." Finally, there is also the *Amici di Gargonza* (Friends of Gargonza) group, which every summer organizes the *Gargonza Estate* (Gargonza Summer), season of artistic and cultural activities. The castello now lives on in the lives of the many people involved in it.

CASTELLO DI STROZZAVOLPE

The rugged, gloomy appearance of days gone by still clings to the Castello di Strozzavolpe. The small drawbridge is now always down, while the door opens only to admit the cars belonging to the owner or the caretaker's family. For the remainder of the time, as in the past, it stays firmly shut. But the castello – whose clean lines can be admired from the small town of Poggibonsi, which links the provinces of Florence and Siena – is not an inhospitable place. It simply chooses to preserve its identity as a fortress, unable to indulge in any form of gallantry. It has retreated behind the pale, reassuring solidity of its stones, the rhythmical geometry of its Guelph merlons, the broad, compact mass of its keep, the human history of its few houses, and the proud, untamed shape of its tower. The only concessions to a less aggressive mood are a small garden of geometric beds and a quiet, unassuming chapel built during the sixteenth century at a time when the echoes of the countless battles that had raged around these walls were gradually fading away.

Many people who own buildings of this sort try to exploit their commercial potential. Some open restaurants in an old outbuilding, some convert the whole thing

Above: Set amid the castello's crenellated walls, the bell of the old chapel has rung out over the centuries. After entering through the gateway, a gentle incline leads into a small courtyard dominated by the powerful mass of the keep.

Opposite: The castello stands in an inaccessible position. From below it is impossible to appreciate its full architectural glory: only an aerial view can do it full justice. From above it is easy to understand how impregnable it is, with its ring of walls firmly entrenched on the top of a hill. It is also easy to see how, given the purity of its lines, it has come to be regarded as one of the finest and best preserved fortresses in Tuscany, a fortified stronghold that is more than a thousand years old.

into a hotel, and others do everything possible to encourage visitors. The owners of Strozzavolpe, however, have refused to adopt any of these courses. Aldo Arcangeli, a lawyer well-known in Florentine professional circles, and his wife, Signora Carla Banchi Bizzarri, are happy just to maintain and embellish the castello. They feel a strong emotional link with this fortress, caring for it as though it were their child and respecting every nook and cranny of its fabric. Cultured and indefatigable custodians of these walls, they have virtually been enslaved by this fascinating stronghold that, once revealed, remains forever in the memory.

Many years ago, Aldo Arcangeli searched the castello's old archives, and in the spirit of a true historian succeeded in reconstructing its history. It is a complex story, involving the endless wars between Siena and Florence and countless changes in ownership, during which the castello belonged to the ancient counts of Barbiano, the conti Alberti di Prato, Vernio e Mongona, the Squarcialupi di Monternana, the Alberti, marchesi of Tuscany, the conti Guidi, the Salimbeni, the Firidolfi di Panzano, the Adimari, the Rinuccini, the Ricciardi, the Franceschi

Left: This small garden softens the severe lines of the castello. The small family chapel, with its elegant late-Renaissance shapes, is dedicated to St Peter of Alcantara, who was a guest in the castello when it was owned by Donati di Antonio Adimari and Alessandra de' Bardi. An attractive example of sixteenth-century architecture, it differs in mood from its surroundings yet blends well with them.

Below: The courtyard, fringed by buildings that formerly housed the garrison but are now home to the caretakers and their family, contains this fine octagonal well head erected at the same time as the castello and thus many centuries old.

della Mercanzia, and the Da Cepparello family, all of them members of the Tuscan nobility.

No documentary evidence for the history of Strozzavolpe prior to 1000 has survived, but at the beginning of the eleventh century it was already a redoubtable stronghold whose position and military strength made it almost impregnable. It was equipped with a large number of trap doors and secret passages, the most famous of which still exists today. A magnificent feat of engineering, it consists of a very long tunnel running beneath the entire length of the valley that provides an escape route from the castello to the bastion of Poggio Imperiale, built on the orders of Emperor Arrigo VII and fortified by the Medici. It was once thought that this was yet another of the many legends surrounding Strozzavolpe, but the discovery of certain sections of it in the area has confirmed its existence. It was Guido Guerra, the adoptive son of Contessa Matilde of Tuscany, who first had the idea of creating this long subterranean link during the dark, turbulent days of the Middle Ages. The conte, a man of few friends who was famous for his ruthless military prowess, used every trick at his disposal to ensure the safety of his men and his own illustrious person.

The tunnel is no legend, but there are clearly a multitude of other tales concerning Strozzavolpe that have sprung from the fertile popular imagination. One of the most intriguing concerns the origins of the name *Strozzavolpe*, which literally means ''strangle-wolf.'' The castello is believed to have been named after some far-distant owners called ''Scoriavolpe,'' but the legendary version is far more interesting. The tale is set during the time of Bonifazio, prince of Tuscany, who may also have been responsible for building the castello. After spotting the rugged hill, he ordered his men to erect a fortress, but they were attacked by a wolf as strong as a lion. A hunt was immediately organized to find and kill the animal, but it was no easy matter: the wolf launched itself against the horsemen from behind every bush, flames shooting from its mouth. The prince therefore resorted to a trick and succeeded in throwing a noose around its neck and throttling it. The court magician prophesized that the cas-

Top: A narrow parapet grants access to the regular Guelph merlons that run round the entire perimeter of the walls. From here the ancient red tiles seem to touch the square block of the keep, while the rolling green countryside in the distance makes a pleasing contrast with the angularity of the walls.

Above: The rear facade of the keep looks over the strict geometric layout of the garden. The tower of the castello stands ever watchful in the background.

tle would last only for as long as it took the body of the wolf to decompose. Bonifazio ingeniously outwitted the prophesy: he had molten gold poured into the animal's body, thus preventing it from ever rotting away. The wolf was then hidden in the castello and revered with due pomp and ceremony. Some centuries later a peasant chanced upon the gilded wolf, but he was immediately confronted by the ghosts of three horsemen who emerged from the woods, attacked him, and hid the body once again.

During the post-medieval period, certain alterations were made to the castello to turn it into a much more elegant residence, although no changes were made to its layout.

A number of famous people have stayed at Strozzavolpe over the years, among them Lorenzo de' Medici, and the Franciscan monk Peter of Alcantara, who during the sixteenth century was the guest of the owners Donato di Antonio Adimari and Alessandra de' Bardi. An exemplary figure in the rectitude and strictness of his life, he is mentioned in the writings of St Teresa of Avila and, like her, he also was canonized. Another man who spent a considerable amount of time at Strozzavolpe was one of the greatest Italian artists of the seventeenth century, Salvator Rosa. An entertaining figure with a multi-faceted personality, Rosa was famous not only for his splendid paintings, but also for his comedies, his practical jokes, his drollery, and the controversial streak that very quickly brought him to prominence in Rome, earning him as many enemies and critics as friends and admirers. This turbulent genius stayed at Strozzavolpe on several occasions between 1659 and 1665, as the friend and guest of the owner of the day, Giovanni Battista Ricciardi.

Aldo Arcangeli is a man of great learning and an avid collector. The area around Strozzavolpe is rich in archaeological remains and on the first floor of the keep a large room contains a display cabinet filled with objects unearthed in the surrounding countryside: Roman tear glasses, ivories, small rings and coins.

A small iron bridge leads into one side of the keep, access to which is gained along the walls, with its very narrow, brick parapet. The lichen-covered tiles on the roofs of the houses form a vast red carpet inhabited by countless snails that warm themselves in the sun before disappearing furtively into the cracks between the stones. It is a scene that has been dominated by the tower since the earliest days. At the garden level, a small loggia supported by two columns contains a number of Roman and Renaissance busts, as well as a fine fourteenth-century statue of St Agnes and an altar, also Roman. A few steps away, encased in the

Above: This portrait bust of Catherine de' Medici, later queen of France, shows a determined, strong-willed woman, a woman born to command.

Opposite: The armoury is laid out along strict, museum-like lines. Rare halberds, jousting lances, suits of armour, hunting swords and shields, both European and Oriental, are now merely objects to be admired.

Below: In the great armoury, the austerity of this grey stone fireplace dating from the sixteenth century is tempered by its decoration of floral swags.

walls, stands the family chapel dedicated to St Peter of Alcantara, a building of pleasing proportions with niches at either side of the door that once contained statues. Within the keep there is a large armoury containing full suits of armour, massive breastplates, halberds and sharp jousting lances of the fifteenth and sixteenth centuries. There are also a number of beautifully fashioned hunting swords, as well as rugged shields, both European and Oriental, pikes and powder flasks, a small arsenal that no longer has to respond to the ancient call to arms.

At either side of a door stand two matching tables. One of these supports a bust of Catherine de' Medici, queen of France, whose strong features and proud, unflinching gaze betray a face that seems to have lost its femininity; the other displays the bust of an unidentified Medici grand duke. The far wall contains a large sixteenth-century stone fireplace.

The nineteenth-century staircase leading to the upper floors is surrounded by a number of fine Roman busts, the most attractive of which is a small portrait of a balding, middle-aged man with a strong face and expressive features, perhaps a Roman emperor. Upstairs there are many rooms, including the one containing the owner's collection of small archaeological finds, the so-called *stanza delle donne medicee*, which houses busts of famous ladies of the Medici family.

The castello's interiors are certainly fine, but it is the walls, the layout, the almost unaltered external appearance that captures our imagination. A castle that is mysterious but not sinister, austere but not unwelcoming, Strozzavolpe still has the power to captivate.

The castello is also a very busy place, whose estate has for centuries produced grain, fodder and excellent wines. For generations the owners of Strozzavolpe have been skilled practitioners of the art of wine making. The rich, fertile land borders the Chianti Classico area, and the wine it produces, when treated with the proper care and attention, can more than hold its own against wines bearing the more famous Gallo Nero label. The estate, relatively small in size, consists of 50 hectares (124 acres), much of which has been laid down to vines. A number of fine labels are produced, such as Bianco di Strozzavolpe, a dry, DOC wine with a strong bouquet. The red wine, also of a very high quality, bears the Chianti Putto denomination, a label that is a sure guarantee of excellence. Another wine produced at Strozzavolpe, albeit in small quantities, is the famous Vin Santo. This wine, which is difficult to make, is typical of Tuscany and is normally served as a dessert wine.

The winery at Strozzavolpe employs a small work force and is almost a family concern. A charming gentleman, almost

Above: A fifteenth-century fresco.

Opposite: The other great room on the upper floor contains a display case holding small archaeological finds, mainly of the Roman era.

Below: The well of the staircase leading up to the upper floors is elegantly decorated with a group of Roman busts.

Signor Arcangeli's right-hand man, is also very knowledgeable on the subject of wine, and it is he who oversees the wines in the cellar, who tastes them and decides whether the time is right or not for bottling. Although the winery employs few people, this is compensated for by a strictly run organization and use of the latest technology.

The lawyer and his wife live in Florence, but every week they travel to Strozzavolpe, happy to glimpse the castello on the horizon as they round a sharp bend. On arriving, they invariably perform what has become a sort of ritual. After passing over the drawbridge, Signora Arcangeli opens the great door with an immense iron key while her husband goes to visit the cellars to greet the workmen and his trusted friend, the wine expert. He conducts a rapid inspection, samples the wine, and then returns to the castello to reimmerse himself in the pleasant routine of daily life.

CASTELLO DI FOSDINOVO

A line of houses stretches over a hill covered in a mantle of bright green that seems to fight for space with the medieval town of Fosdinovo and its maze of alleys and intersecting streets. A small town, or rather a citadel, it is supported in its age-old struggle with the hill by a solid giant clinging to the highest point of its rugged mass.

The Castello Malaspina at Fosdinovo is of a type not often found in Tuscany. Apart from looking more like an aristocratic northern Italian castle, it also displays features reminiscent of non-Italian buildings. An imposing block of tightly grouped buildings, it creates an impression of great strength. By night, when the castello is floodlit from below, it appears from a distance as a great splash of light in the darkness; viewed at closer range it is revealed as an edifice of rare and powerfully evocative beauty, with a subtle charm at once both crude and sophisticated. It is like the typical toy fortress of a small child's dreams.

The inhabitants of this remote town are really mountain folk, despite the fact that the sea is only a short distance away. These are people whose lives have always revolved around their castle: it is part of

Above: The castello stands on a hill dominating the valley. Around it, groves of chestnut trees embrace the rough stone walls.

Opposite: The parapets, reinforced by internal walls, are those of a large castle. Below, we catch a glimpse of the courtyard, extensively altered during the sixteenth century, and the door with its marble surround, through which visitors enter. This leads into a seemingly endless series of rooms of every sort. These walls once protected the most powerful lords of the beautiful region known as the Lunigiana.

their identity, a steadfast friend rooted deep in their subconscious. They refer to it as though it were a living thing, handing down stories and legends about it from one generation to the next.

While the castello could thus be said to have about five hundred owners (the number of people living in the town), its true owners are the marchesi Torrigiani Malaspina, an old Florentine family. The marchese Vieri, who is delighted to explain to visitors the history behind every corner of his domain, is a born storyteller, weaving interesting and magical tales with just the right emphasis. Fosdinovo is strategically located on the boundary between Tuscany and Liguria, where one can almost touch the Gulf of La Spezia, and clearly glimpse the outskirts of the attractive town of Sarzana, with the delightful resorts of Portovenere and Lerici only a short distance away. This unique position was recognized in the early eleventh century, when building work began on the castello. Fosdinovo is mentioned in documents dating from the early years of the thirteenth century, but by then it had almost certainly already been standing for some time. It was not until 1340, however, when the powerful

marchese Spinetta Malaspina acquired the domain, that it was extensively fortified and enlarged. Further alterations made by Spinetta's grandson, Galeotto Malaspina, brought it up to its present size, and it was this great family that continued to dominate the region until the end of the eighteenth century.

There was originally a drawbridge, but visitors now enter the castello directly through the old gateway into a fine courtyard known as the *piazzetta dei cannoni*, which is based on a series of elliptical arches with low, broadly spaced marble pillars and Romanesque capitals composed of square-shaped foliate elements. The apertures for the cannons are still there; but these instruments of death have gone and now all is peace.

Accompanying the marchese Vieri on visitors' tours is Daniele Bonotti, a young architecture student who is the son of the family who looks after the castello when the marchesi are away. A striking example of how attached the people of Fosdinovo are to the castello, Daniele knows all there is to know about it. Having studied all the documents, he has gathered a fund of information that he imparts with the eagerness of a true enthusiast.

Arriving at the central courtyard, one's first impression is confirmed: certain stylistic details, such as those of the arcade and the sixteenth-century loggia, and even the colour of the stone, seem

Left: Seen from one of the bastions of its castello, Fosdinovo appears as a maze of densely packed houses stretched out along the hill. The town has always lived in close contact with the castello, through good times and bad.

Center: The powerful shape of the bastion contrasts with the unexpected patch of green provided by a rustic hanging garden among the stone.

Bottom: The broad expanse of the sixteenth-century courtyard, with its elegant loggia of sweeping columns and its fine portico blocking off the medieval walls, represents a happy marriage between the rugged stone structure of a fortress and the softer architecture of a sixteenth-century residence.

Opposite: After leaving the courtyard, visitors pass through a marble doorway that leads into the entrance hall, whose elegant ceiling features a fine decorative motif depicting a dolphin's head and a flowering thorn, symbols of the ancient family of Malaspina. The hall also contains items of sixteenth-century armour and, against the far wall, a splendid travelling trunk that once belonged to Valentina Visconti, wife of Duke Louis of Orléans.

many rooms and corridors that, without a guide, one could easily get lost and risk falling through one of the countless trapdoors hidden throughout the castello.

When visitors enter the dining room, the marchese invariably apologizes for its sparseness explaining that his property has been a frequent target of thieves. What is still there, however, is more than enough to give the interior a feeling of grandeur that echoes the power once enjoyed by the fiefdom of Fosdinovo. The room contains a fine, rather austere refectory table, a stone fireplace and a set of period chairs. There is also a cabinet displaying a beautiful selection of ceramics dating from the fifteenth to the eighteenth centuries, made at Doccia and Montelupo, towns famous throughout history for the manufacture of such wares.

Another room that should on no account be overlooked is the simple throne room, where a seventeenth-century wrought-iron strong box boasts a complicated locking system involving a great many keys that would challenge even the most seasoned safe breaker. The room also contains the punch once used for striking coins, a privilege granted only to the most powerful and highly respected feudal lords.

According to some historians, Dante was a guest of the castello, and there is even a small room in which this famous poet is said to have slept. If one is to

uncharacteristic of a Tuscan castello. The eye is drawn to a magnificent doorway, made entirely of pure white marble with classical capitals, leading into the interior. The large entrance hall, whose vaulted ceiling is decorated with a motif incorporating a dolphin's head and a flowering thorn (symbols of the Malaspina family), houses items of sixteenth-century armour and a travelling trunk of the same period that once belonged to the beautiful Valentina Visconti, wife of Duke Louis of Orléans. There are so

Above: Tuscany had a proud tradition of majolica and porcelain manufacture and its wares are still in great demand today. These shelves display pieces made in towns that have long been famous throughout the world for their ceramics: Montelupo for its majolica and Doccia for its porcelain.

Opposite: The dining room is restrained and unostentatious, with a simple rectangular table and chairs in the medieval style and a relatively modern fireplace based on Renaissance models. The vaulted ceiling, with its elegant heraldic decoration, encloses the room in a pleasingly symmetrical rhythm.

believe tradition, however, Dante visited almost every place in Tuscany, and conflicting dates would indicate that he never passed through Fosdinovo, although the story nevertheless adds to the appeal of the castello. This and other stories are related in a series of frescoes running along the walls of the vast Great Hall, which makes an ideal setting for parties and receptions. The unusual frescoes are freely inspired by fourteenth-century Florentine painting, but were in fact created by one Gaetano Bianchi, a Florentine decorative artist of the nineteenth century who worked in the castello in 1882. Another fine feature of this room is its cross-vaulted ceiling, which instils a mood of authority and grandeur.

There are too many rooms in the castello to mention each individually, but the *sala ducale* contains a striking portrait of the young Aloisio Malaspina, product of a marriage between one of the lords of Fosdinovo and a girl from the Beccaria family. The child, in a large and splendid green costume (almost like the uniform of a hussar), has piercing black eyes, a broad forehead, and an already proud expression proclaiming his awareness that he will one day grow up to be a Malaspina of Fosdinovo.

One of the castello's massive bastions is softened by a sloping lawn that affords a breathtaking view over the surrounding countryside. Outside, the parapets once

Above: The family coat of arms – a flowering thorn sprouting from a dolphin's head – is here depicted in stone.

Opposite: The poet Dante, beset by political problems that forced him to adopt the life of a wanderer, is said to have been a guest at the Castello di Fosdinovo. The walls of this magnificent room recount the details of his possibly apocryphal stay. The style of the frescoes, clearly inspired by fourteenth-century models, is deceptive; they were actually executed during the nineteenth century, by the Florentine artist Gaetano Bianchi, who was also responsible for the striking equestrian portrait of the marchese Spinetta Malaspina the "Great" on the far wall, in which the turreted mass of his famous castle is clearly visible in the background. The hall, of truly massive proportions, has a charming cross-vaulted ceiling decorated in the neo-Gothic taste. The old wrought-iron lamp hanging from the ceiling casts strangely shaped shadows and long streaks of light that emphasize the haunting quality of this great room.

used by sentries run along almost the whole length of the walls, while the Ghibelline merlons slice the air with their jagged points. From here one can grasp the sophisticated geometry of the castello: a rhythmical mass of roofs and tiles that slopes uninterruptedly down from the courtyard, while beyond the walls lie woods of chestnuts, firs and plume-like cypresses, a sea of green that heaves and rolls as the wind blows through it.

Many ghost stories are associated with the castello. Some people maintain that sleep is impossible in one bedroom on the upper floor because of a clammy invisible presence that chills the bed and the room. This unearthly note increases the fascination of Fosdinovo, which was once a castle belonging to feudal lords but is now home to a gracious Florentine family.

To turn one's back on this majestic complex, with its four turreted bastions that seem like enormous stone pillars sunk into the hill, its simple, restrained rooms that make no concessions to elegance, and its proud, imperious air, is rather like breaking off in the middle of a beautiful tale. Below, in the town, the houses of Fosdinovo seem to cluster even more tightly around their castle when, in the first shadows of late afternoon, their outlines begin to soften and everything disappears beneath a veil of mist that rises up from the valley and envelops the surrounding countryside.

INDEX

INDEX